Adeline Riggs Egbert

Rowland W. Rider at Lee's Ferry—Fall of 1909

SIXSHOOTERS

AND

SAGEBRUSH

Cowboy Stories

of the Southwest

Rowland W. Rider
as told to
Deirdre Paulsen

Brigham Young
University
Press

Library of Congress Cataloging in Publication Data

Rider, Rowland W 1890–
Sixshooters and sagebrush.

1. Rider, Rowland W., 1890– 2. Frontier and pioneer life–Utah–Kanab region. 3. Frontier and pioneer life–Grand Canyon region. 4. Cowboys–Utah–Kanab region–Biography. 5. Cowboys–Grand Canyon region–Biography 6. Folk-lore–Utah–Kanab region. 7. Folklore–Grand Canyon region. 8. Kanab region, Utah–Social life and customs. 9. Grand Canyon region–Social life and customs. I. Paulsen, Deirdre, 1945– II. Title.
F834.K36R527 979.1'3 79-15715
ISBN 0-8425-1696-4

International Standard Book Number: 0-8425-1696-4

Brigham Young University Press, Provo, Utah 84602

79 2Mp 39065

In these latter days of rampant enlightenment, when even professors of English literature contend for computer time, it is good now and then to remind ourselves that there is still a small place in folk scholarship for the not only accurate but articulate human observer—not only the illiterate informant whose reminiscences never leave our archives except in the form of statistics, but those eminently literate persons whose memories of lives begun in folk societies can give us not only understanding of such cultures but sheer gladness in the telling. There are few Hamlin Garlands left, and ere the days of their pilgrimage vanish, we must encourage them to tell us in their eloquence just how it was in those days, gone forever.

John Greenway

Contents

Foreword

I first met Rowland Rider at the home of a colleague, where he had come, escorted by his granddaughter Deirdre Paulsen, to tell "cowboy stories" to an assorted group of BYU English Department faculty members and spouses. As our host's basement-family room gradually filled with new arrivals and as talk flitted easily from the latest departmental gossip to the vagaries of suburban living, I watched Mr. Rider seated straight and uncomfortable on the edge of his chair, far removed, it seemed to me, from the time, place and spirit of the Arizona Strip he was to tell us about—and I wondered what the evening held in store for both him and us.

I needn't have worried. "I want to tell you a funny story," he began, rising to his full heighth. Then he laughed, a laugh so infectious that in short order we were all laughing with him, in spite of the fact that we had not yet heard his story. Two hours later we were still laughing. But in the interim that rough strip of land, which divides Utah and Arizona and which maintained its raw frontier character long after the frontier had disappeared elsewhere, had come vividly alive for us, his enthusiastic listeners.

Perhaps the most remarkable thing about the stories Mr. Rider told that evening was their unity. Though each story was capable of standing alone as a separate tale, the entire group of tales, taken together, formed an integrated and uniform whole. Mr. Rider achieved this unity partly through consistency in tone and narrative style but mostly through an interlocking technique whereby he would present in one story a character or event which he would then use in other tales. For example, the gambling cowboy, Highpockets, appeared in one story almost incidentally, but then showed up a few stories later as one of the leading characters, now already known to the listener from his earlier shenanigans. Similarly, The Roll-Away-Saloon, the nemesis of the local Relief Society sisters but the delight of its cowboy patrons, who rolled it from one side of the Utah-Arizona border to the other to escape the law, was fitted into a story wherever the plot needed it.

Through this interlocking device, Mr. Rider was able to create for us that evening a believable cast of characters, from Jim Emett the cattle thief to the idle cowboys in Kanab whittling the streets full of shavings. Perhaps more important, he was also able to create an engaging and believable picture of the joys and hardships of cowboy life on the Arizona Strip just after the turn of the century. In short, the unity in his stories was a reflection of the unity he had perceived in the cowboy life of his youth and had tried to depict for us.

Rowland Rider's stories, those told at that storytelling session some years ago and those recorded in this book by his granddaughter, can both delight and instruct. Perhaps the scholars most interested in these stories will be oral historians and folklorists.

Until recently, oral historians–historians who record the happenings of the past directly from the people who experienced them–have focused primarly on those famous men and women who have played significant roles in shaping past events. More recently they have begun recording the stories of the common men and women who have lived through these events. Such a man was Rowland Rider. His memories of running cattle in the Kaibab Forest, on the Arizona Strip, and on the rim of the Grand Canyon provide a close personal view of a period of our history which we can scarcely get in other ways.

Yet if we are to use his stories for historical reconstruction we must do so with caution. Mr. Rider's excellent eye for detail and his constant attempts to document and verify the events he describes lend his stories of these events a credibility such accounts often lack. Still we must remember that memory usually does at least two things. It selectively chooses to remember those happenings that have special significance to an individual; and, through the years, it often embellishes these happenings, making them larger than life. As a result, storytelling often becomes an attempt by the teller to characterize the past in terms meaningful to him in the present.

Whether Mr. Rider has added details to his stories as he has told and retold them over the years, I have no way of knowing. But there is no doubt that he has carefully chosen the events he relates from what must have been a much larger storehouse. From his long and productive life, rich with a variety of experiences, he has chosen almost all his stories from that ten-year period when he worked as a cowboy. And from that cowboy period of time he has further chosen to tell only stories which, as his granddaughter points out, serve as a vehicle for his personal philosophy. The world that emerges from these stories is a much harder world than most of us know today, but it is at the same time a much simpler one where an individual can be reasonably sure that if he obeys the rules he will prevail. Nature, animals, and man can all destroy. But nature treated with admiration and careful respect can sustain one; animals treated with both firmness and kindness can support one; and men treated squarely and honestly can become one's helpers and friends.

Whether or not such a world ever really existed is for the historian to say. But for Rowland Rider there is no doubt about its existence. It is his vision of this world that helps sustain him in the more complex and devious society in which he must now live.

Until recently most folklorists would have expressed only passing interest in Mr. Rider's stories, claiming that though a few of them have analogues elsewhere, most are personal experience narratives rather than the oft-told tales the folklorist generally seeks and studies. But just as oral historians have recently begun collecting experiences of the common folk, so too have folklorists begun paying more attention to personal experience stories.

There are a number of reasons for this. First, though Mr. Rider's stories may not be authentic folk narratives themselves, they do carry other kinds of folklore in them—for example, a rich store of cowboy folk speech and numerous descriptions of cowboy customs. Second, folklorists have come to realize that while the experiences a person tells may be unique to himself, the narrative forms he chooses to filter these experiences through are dictated by tradition. They thus shape stories like those told by Mr. Rider into typical-sounding tall tales, legends, and folk anecdotes, which, if told often enough, may indeed pass into oral tradition and become authentic folklore. Third, the principles involved in oral performance are essentially the same whether the story told is a personal experience or a traditional tale. Folklorists today are devoting at least as much study to the art of telling a story as they are to the story told, realizing that the art of a narrative lies more in its performance than in its appearance on the printed page, however faithfully recorded. Anyone who has watched Mr. Rider perform, has seen him get down on hands and knees to imitate a bull, or has watched him draw listeners into his stories through facial expressions, gestures, and mimicry knows what it is to witness a masterful storyteller.

Storytellers like Mr. Rider become in time what Richard M. Dorson has called sagamen. "Sometimes," says Dorson, "a fluent storyteller launches into a stream of highly colored personal experiences that enthrall his audience as much or more than any folk tale. In his autobiographical sagas he plays a heroic role, overmastering the hazards and outwitting the dangers presented by vicious men, ferocious beasts, and implacable nature. These narratives rest on explicit factual detail and yet they are strongly flavored with romance" (Richard M. Dorson, *Bloodstoppers and Bearwalkers: Folk Traditions of the Upper Peninsula* [Cambridge: Harvard University Press, 1952], p. 249). As time passes, the sagaman creates his own legend, or, as is the case with Mr. Rider, his own oral literary masterpiece. For Mr. Rider has told his stories to so many people on so many occasions, and has told them so well, that, taken as a whole, they have become what literature in general is conceded to be–an artistic rendering of significant human experience.

And perhaps herein lies the principal value of these stories. As noted earlier, they have become a sort of objective correlative for what Mr. Rider perceives life to have been on the Arizona Strip at the turn of the century. To be sure, they give a valuable picture of the style of life on the Strip at that time, but they give a still more valuable and moving picture of the man who experienced that life and who, through scores of different circumstances and for nearly seventy years, has kept it in his heart ever since, using it whenever necessary to maintain his balance in a world not always of his own liking. Telling stories is one of the devices people use to manipulate their environment to their own advantage. Through telling his stories, Mr. Rider has been able to maintain a strong sense of identification with the land of his youth and a continued commitment to the values he associates with that land.

William A. Wilson

Introduction

Rowland Rider is an irrepressible teller of cowboy stories. In the early 1900s he was a cowboy in the Arizona Strip-Grand Canyon area, an area where range wars were a way of life, guns were used to settle arguments, and the penalty for cattle rustling was hanging. It was the time and place of Zane Grey's inspiration, of Teddy Roosevelt's visits to the Grand Canyon, of Julius F. Stone's courageous exploration of the Colorado River–an era following on the heels of Butch Cassidy, the Robber's Roost gang, and John D. Lee's exile at Lonely Dell. Rider knows and recalls these times.

Rider was born in 1890, the last of thirteen children born to early Mormon settlers John and Mary McDonald Rider of Kanab, Utah. John Rider had been sent by Brigham Young in 1870 to help fortify this isolated town on the Utah-Arizona border against Indian attack. In 1895, when Rowland was five, John Rider was appointed a district judge in Millcreek, Salt Lake County, Utah. John left his cattle interests under the management of his older sons and, together with his wife, four sons, and four daughters, he made the 360-mile journey north to Salt Lake over rough trails, "traveling in two covered wagons, with three teams of horses and four saddle horses."

Rowland attended grade school and high school in Salt Lake City and was active in sports and drama. In October 1907 his father sold the farm and orchard in Millcreek and returned to his cattle interests in Kanab. Prior to the move he told Rowland "to invest in a complete cowboy outfit, hat to spurs, and the best saddle available in the city." And so began Rider's career as a cowboy.

For the next three years Rider worked full time as a cowboy in the Utah-Arizona border country, mostly on the Kaibab Plateau north of the Grand Canyon. He stated that he visited town rarely but was never bored because "exciting action occurred almost daily." That "exciting action" is the marrow of this collection.

In 1910 Rider decided to go to college. He enrolled in the two-year engineering course at the Branch Agricultural College (now the College of Southern Utah) in Cedar City, Utah, but he returned each summer to help his brothers with the family's cattle interests. Rider records that much spiritual growth occurred while he was living in Cedar City, for he lived in the home of Bishop William Corey, who had been a bishop of The Church of Jesus Christ of Latter-day Saints (Mormon) for twenty-five years.

In September 1912, having finished at Cedar City, Rowland enrolled in the Agricultural College in Logan, Utah (now Utah State University) and studied engineering for the next three-and-a-half years. Each summer he returned to Kanab and the life of a cowboy. He met Romania Fawcett in June 1916 and the two were married a year later. They honeymooned in Los Angeles and returned by car over the two-track Arrowhead Trail. They were among the first to make that harrowing trip by car. Rowland joined the wartime army in 1918, but he was discharged following the armistice after only a fifteen-month, rather uneventful enlistment.

Rider spent the next ten years prospecting for ore, hunting in the Kaibab Forest and working in Kanab. He surveyed, served as city marshal, carved the church cornerstone, built a power plant, and installed electricity in Kanab. He owned an automobile garage in Kanab, and, as a result, he spent a lot of time rescuing stranded motorists in the desert.

In 1928 Rider sold his garage and moved his family to Salt Lake City, where they remained. By that time Rowland and Romania had three children: Ramona, Max, and Bert.

Since his cowboy years Rowland has been an engineer and inventor. He has worked for the Remington Arms Manufacturing Company, the Atomic Energy Commission, and has recently retired from the Rider Engineering and Plastic Company, a firm he founded. He has many inventions to his credit, from a rotary engine, which he developed in 1927, to the "intracath," a disposable intravenous device he developed for Deseret Pharmaceutical Company.

In 1919 Rider, on leave from the army, met John Willy, the editor of *Hotel Monthly,* who was recording one of the first automobile trips to the Grand Canyon. Rider helped Willy repair his car, and that evening Willy chanced to hear Rider telling stories at the Marysvale Inn, in Marysvale, Utah. Willy records:

As it was getting dark, we all put up at the Grand Hotel, and after supper, sitting on the hotel porch, conversation drifted to desert life, 'the riders of the purple sage.' Then it was we learned that the driver of the Oldsmobile truck had been a 'rider.' He was a 'son of the desert': and was acquainted with Zane Grey, the author, in fact had suggested to Mr. Grey ideas for some of his wonderful desert stories. He told of the buffalo ranch near Kanab; of the deer, wild horses, cougar, and other wild animal life of the Kaibab Forest; of his being the last man to bid God speed to two intrepid explorers of Grand Canyon as they started downstream for the Granite Gorge from Lee's Ferry; ... his language simple and direct, without waste of words ... and breathed of sincerity. He was a most interesting man.

Willy further described Rider as being a "keen looking, athletic young fellow in smart soldier uniform." He referred to him having an "eagle eye" and that "he had come across the desert and up the hill so fast the jackrabbits hardly had time to get out of his way."

During the intervening years Rowland Rider has loved telling stories. Tall and slim, and usually wearing cowboy boots and a tall cowboy hat, Rider naturally attracts a following. Children ask where his horse is, and tourists delay their buses. In October 1976 Utah folklorist Bert Wilson recommended Rider as the "best storyteller in these parts," and Rider was asked to participate in the annual National Storytelling Festival at Jonesboro, Tennessee (sponsored by the National Association for the Preservation and Perpetuation of Storytelling). There he was featured in the local papers and televison and was taped and interviewed by National Public Radio.

Rider still tells his stories at every opportunity. Even though each storytelling situation and each storytelling audience is unique, Rider seems to follow a basic storytelling pattern. Usually beginning with a humorous story to relax and "loosen up" his audience he states: "Now I'm going to tell you a funny one—this is one you'll never believe." And as he swings into the story, emphasizing points by slapping his thighs and knees, and laughing—often so hard that he's gasping by the time he again picks up the thread of the story—he soon has even a "cold" audience laughing with him.

After Rider becomes comfortable with his audience, he uses gestures to further increase his rapport—enfolding his audience, breaking down the conversational distance, and forcing their eyes to focus on him. All the major points of each tale are emphasized through gestures. During exciting action he is in continuous movement. In the story "Buffalo Jones 'Outbuffalos' a Buffalo," Rider often kneels on the floor and swings his arms down and back to portray the buffalo pawing the ground.

Very rarely does an audience question the truthfulness of Rider's stories. This may be due to his elaborate introductions and conclusions, and his use of specific detail. In addition, he looks the part of a cowboy, and he uses idiomatic cowboy expressions and cowboy grammar. He is earnest in his delivery, and he has an obvious love for his subject.

Rider's cowboy years lasted only ten years, yet those years have been central in his life, and have shaped his philosophy of rugged independence. Pragmatism has been important in Rider's professional life, but religious dedication, love for the range, and love of nature–coupled with a spontaneous sense of humor–influence his stories, and have been the primary influence in his personal life.

Rider telling stories in the Kaibab Forest–1970

Part One

At Home on the Range

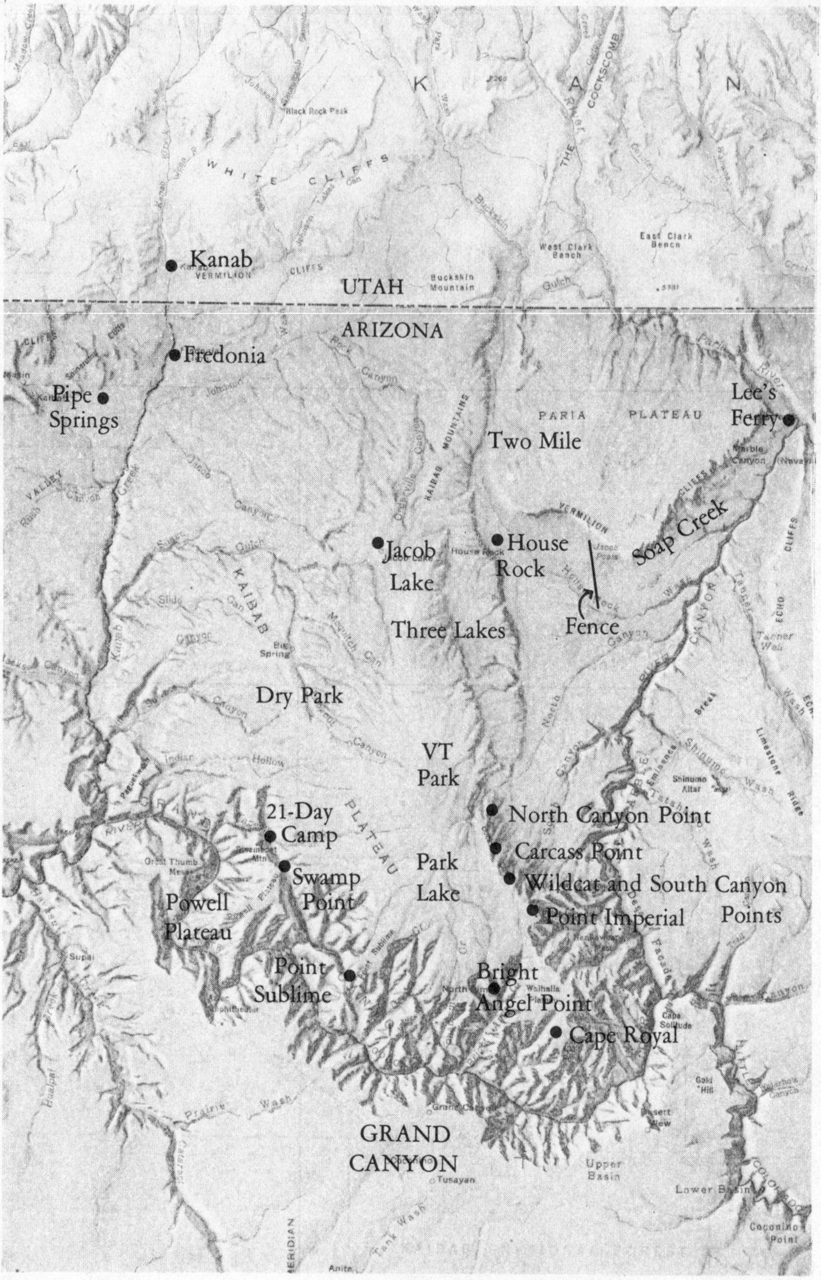

The Utah-Arizona Border Area
Scene of Rider's cowboy experiences

The Roll Away Saloon

This is quite a notorious story on the Arizona Strip because it involves liquor. As far as I can remember, all the cowboys liked to drink alcohol. Oh, boy, they'd drink home brewed, they'd drink lemon extract and vanilla extract. The freighters couldn't get it in there fast enough. The stores would sell out right away. That's a fact.

So they built this little saloon and it was right on the Arizona-Utah line four miles south of Kanab and four miles north of Fredonia about seven or eight rods to the west of the present highway. It was just kind of a two-room affair, with a bar at one end and the barkeeper's bedroom at the other end. It wasn't very large, maybe twelve by eighteen feet, but it created quite a bit of disturbance among the Mormon housewives of Fredonia and Kanab because their men would come staggering up home on their horses, too late for dinner, unable to take their saddles off. So the men of these towns, fearing their women, built this saloon on rollers, log rollers that went clear under the joist.

Well, one day when the women in the Relief Society up to Kanab got together sewing and having a quilting bee, they decided among themselves that too many of their men were going down imbibing at this Roll Away Saloon. So they organized a posse to go and burn the thing down. And their plans were all kept a secret from their husbands, of course. So when the men all went out on the range or out in the fields or doing something, the women saddled up their horses, a lot of them rode, and some of them took their white-tops[1] and they headed for this saloon.

Just fortunately for the saloon keeper there, there's a little raise of land to the north about a quarter mile from the saloon, and on the south side there's also a little incline up to a little ridge there, what we call Halfway Hill. And sure enough, this saloon keeper saw the dust coming from these women on horseback and these four or five white-tops as they came over the rise. And he got the crowbar and rolled the saloon back into Arizona. The women got down there and were all ready to light their torches, they had their bundles all ready,

[1]Four wheels with a framework like a small covered wagon. Wooden benches, enough to seat several people, were added.

when the saloon keeper said, "You can't touch this business; it's in Arizona. We don't belong to Utah at all. There's the line."

It was well paved, the line was, and it always had been. So they had a little confab, then said to the saloon keeper, "Well, if you sell our men any more liquor, we'll get you next time." So they went back home all disgusted that they couldn't go over into Arizona and wreck that place, and went back to their quilting.

Well, anyway, in a few days or a few weeks maybe, why the women down in Fredonia would be doing the same thing, quilting and making things for the needy and so forth. They would find out that their husbands had been spending all the spare cash up there at the Roll Away Saloon, so they'd organize a posse and here they would come. They'd come over that little ridge down there a quarter mile from the saloon and the saloon keeper'd see them coming, and it'd just take a few little pushes on those crowbars under the logs under the saloon, and over she'd go, over into Utah. The women would come up and the same thing would happen. "You can't touch me, I'm over here in Utah. Look there, there's the line." So the women would give up, threatening, and go back to Fredonia. And this went on for years.

Well, now, that's the Roll Away Saloon story and I guess I'm the only one that ever told it. And I think if you want to take a picture, you might find a few of those old rollers still rotting over there.

S'n'Ostrich

Well, I'll tell you one more funny little story. We had these roundups in the spring in which all the cowmen in the country joined. It was necessary because it was a common drive and the territory was tremendous. We started up under the red ledges up there at Kanab and went all the way over to the Paria. We would drive these cattle, but they had been driven year after year so all you had to do was dash up to a bunch of them and hit your chaps with your quirt and let out a few war whoops and give them a start in the right direction. All those trails went like a tree backwards from the watering holes, branching out as they went. So all we had to do was ride the head of those trails and give the cattle a boot and there they would go. And you could see the dust for miles because of the cattle going toward Pipe Springs where the turnover was made, where the buyers came to buy the cattle.[2] And that old Roll Away Saloon was there on the way.

I had as my riding partner that day, next to me, a cowboy from Missouri. His name was Amos, but he was the slowest man in the world and we all called him "Swift." He'd light a cigarette and before he would take the second puff it would be burned down so that he couldn't puff the second time. Well, Swift turns to me and says, "I've got to get a drink, Rowland." And I says, "Come on, Amos, you can't do it. We've got to keep the end of our line up." And he says, "It won't take me a minute. I haven't had one for months." I knew that this was true because he had been in the outfit that long and there was no liquor. So I says, "All right, if you'll only take one so that we can join the rest in the line." We went in and I went with him to see that he didn't stay too long and he drank one and put it down and drank another one before I could get hold of his arm. I said, "Come on, Swift. We have got to go." But by the time he got in his chaps to get the money out, why we'd got behind a little bit and so we jogged along.

About a mile from the saloon there was a colony, and there has been for many years, a colony of ground owls, beautiful owls about the size of a pigeon with little ears and they look just like Siamese cats, except they have a beak instead of the cat's nose, and they got the ears stickin' up there and a big round face and, oh, boy, they are beautiful things. They build their nests in the springtime in the badger holes. The badger drills down there about three feet and it's there these owls nest. They build their nest down in these badger holes and the female sits on the eggs down in there, but the male sits on top and he's the guard, seeing that no rattlesnakes or anything can get down there to interfere with his mate hatching the eggs. And if you come over there he won't fly or run, he just sits there and dares you. He turns right around and just looks at you.

Well, we rode along and there was a lot of them along there and time we got out there about a quarter of a mile, Amos leaned over his saddle as he saw one of those things and says, "T'is it?" Well he meant "What is it?" so I knew his tongue was getting thick. I says,

---

[2]Then the buyers would put the cattle on the railroad at Lund, Utah and ship them to Los Angeles.

"It's an owl." And he says, "S'not n'owl, 's'n'eagle." In his condition he thought it was too big to be an owl, so it had to be an eagle.

And he rode closer and I can still see him looking over his horse on that warm spring day, looking toward that thing. Well I guess the poor owl finally lost his nerve because he ducked back down into his hole, and old Swift said as he saw that ground owl bury himself, "'Snot 'neagle, 'sneither, 's'n'ostrich."

Ground Owls

Well, you know, I had seen these little owls for so long riding in that area that whenever I did I would respect their nests, and I would turn my horse out around them, and naturally you would, and everytime I would do that they would look at me. And they'd look at me here in front and as I went along they'd turn their heads and keep lookin' at me.

So one day I thought I'd do this for an experiment. I rode toward this little ground owl and when he saw me, why he put his head up and watched, you know, and I rode along there with him watching me. And I was real careful because I didn't want to run over him. I rode around there again and he kept watching me and I rode around again making circles around him. He kept watching me come around and I went around three times and his head fell off.

Betting Gold Pieces

This'n's a wild cowboy story. No one will believe this. Those cowboys in Kanab had nothing to do. They didn't have a saloon, you know, because their wives would go down there and roll it back into Arizona. So they'd set around and whittle. I'm not kidding you, there was three or four inches of shavings all over everywhere up and down that main street. These men would sit around the post office, most of them waiting for the stage; we didn't have automobiles, we had a stagecoach pulled by four horses, and on a buckboard because it was five spoke sand from Kanab to Mt. Carmel over the sand dunes. (I don't know whether you know what five spoke sand is. That means if you've got a wagon wheel and you're pulling it through the sand, that the sand would touch five spokes on the periphery of that wheel. And that's the way it is on the way to Kanab—there's sand dunes across there.) These fellows once a year maybe would get some mail from the stage just before tax time and probably on Christmas. So these men would whittle to pass the time . . . and would bet, bet on anything you can think of. They would bet gold. And one time the betting was on how far a horse I was riding jumped when he was bucking.

Eck Findlay owned this particular horse. Eck was a cattleman, one of the wealthiest down there. We brought his horse in on the Fourth of July for the rodeo. A bunch of us went out and rounded up a wild band so we'd have horses to ride and we brought him in with this wild band. He had Eck's brand on him. He'd branded him when he was a colt, but he was a stallion now and wild and had quite a few mares with him in that big herd. Eck decided he'd make a saddle horse out of him and I said to him, "Eck, that horse will never make a saddle horse." And he said, "Oh, yes, he's a good horse, good blood." And he hired Bud Wilson, the professional bronco buster, to break him.

Practically every man in Kanab would turn their horses to Wilson to break. He had so much business that he had his corral full of horses all the time. He had been a bronco buster a long while, was well-adapted to it. In fact, he'd ridden so long he was bowlegged. He had to ride a horse ten times before he could earn his twenty-five dollars. That's all they paid him to break a bronco. The horse had to be trained to the hackamore only, not the bridle, just the hackamore—and had to stand still while you hobbled him, and had to receive the saddle. And then Wilson had to learn him to swing on his hind legs back and forth.

One day after we had brought this horse in, Wilson was riding him and it was about the third time that he'd ridden him. He rode him uptown to see how the whittlers were getting along and then turned around and went out of town and was going down by my brother Dave's place. I was there helping him put the feed boxes in the barn. All of a sudden, we heard this horse squealing and we felt the ground trembling. We come out of the barn and we looked up over a little orchard of peach trees my brother had down there along the road inside the fence. There were about three or four rows of peaches and they were young trees but they were up eight or ten feet.

at least. And we could see above these peach trees this Bud Wilson going up and down over there. He went high, I'll tell you. Well, all of a sudden, this Bud Wilson just kept on going and the horse went down in front of my brother's home and turned east on the road to his range where he was raised just as fast as he could go with Wilson's saddle and hackamore.

Well, I had a good horse, the only palomino in the country at that time, a big, tall fellow. And he was trained so that when I'd whistle, he'd come. This day he was out in a little alfalfa field there next to my brother's orchard with some of my brother's other saddle horses. And he heard this squealing and he was excited. So I whistled and he came and I just held the bridle out—I didn't have time to saddle him because I wanted to catch that horse right away and get Bud's outfit—and he grabbed the bit and I slipped it over his ears. My brother run and opened the gate. When that horse started running I grabbed his mane and leaped right on. We took after that stallion and drove eight miles on a fast run. I caught him at Cedar Ridge. He was given out and running down and he didn't think anyone was after him, I guess. I rode alongside of him and picked up the hackamore rope. He'd been trained to be snubbed, so I just took him in a circle since there were no fences. I just let him keep running and finally changed directions and come back to Kanab, slowed down, of course, and come in on a walk.

When I arrived in town I was really tickled; half the town had come out to meet me to see whether I'd caught the stallion or not. They didn't think anybody ever could. Bud was riding bareback behind someone else. He was sure glad to get his outfit back, but said, "I never want to see that horse again. Eck, I wouldn't ride him, I'd kill him first." And so Eck Findlay says to me, he said, "Rowl, do you want to finish breaking him? I have seven more rides comin' to me, so that's all you've got to do, just ride him seven times." I says, "Okay, I'll do it."

I took him down to my corral and because I knew he'd been broke to lead and saddle, I put my outfit on him, saddle and hackamore. Along with the hackamore was always a six- or eight-foot rope that you used to tie the horse up to the tying post or held to when you was sitting on your haunches. Mine had a big knot at the end made of rawhide that Orson Hamblin, a little fellow, a little dwarf who was an expert on making rawhide ropes, had woven.

Lucky I had had him weave that on the end because that knot saved my life that very day.

Well, I decided to try the stallion out, and he went along fine. I was watching for him, though, because I knew that he had taken Bud unawares, so I kept alert. And he went out of town all right and went right on down south toward the Roll Away Saloon, passed it up and went right on down into the White Sage flats below. I was giving him a good workout, going along at a nice big gallop down the grade there towards the little town of Fredonia, when we came to all these trails that all came into one big trail where the horse and cattle went to water. And that horse apparently had come, over the past years, in there to water. When he came to those trails where they crossed the road, he stopped of his own accord and he threw his head up in the air and he whistled. I don't know if you've ever heard a mustang, or a stallion especially, whistle. You can hear them a mile. They just bulge up their chest and they let loose. Then he broke to the right on this trail toward the creek and he started to buck and boy, did he buck.

I didn't expect he was going to buck. I'd never been thrown but I knew I had to really ride that time because I'd seen him throw the best cowhand in the country, that professional bronco buster. I stuck and I stuck to him until he stepped in a badger hole. His front feet went down one of those and he went end for end and I went the end of that eight-foot rope that had the knot in it. That horse when he come up wheeled around and come right at me but I was up on my feet by then. He come right at me striking, and he grabbed with his great big old teeth and then he'd strike. He'd rear up and strike and squeal and the only thing I could do was take that knot, give it a little leeway, and when he'd strike I'd hit. I knew I had to knock his eyes out or he'd kill me, so I knocked out his left eye first because I was right-handed. I got that out but that didn't even slow him down at all.

Now I had a time getting that other eye, though. Boy, I thought I was a goner several times. If I had stumbled or anything, there wouldn't have been anything left. He would've just tromped me to pieces, which I had seen them wild horses do, not to men, but to other horses. I finally got the other eye out but even then I didn't dare go near him. Anytime I'd move he could hear me and he'd rear and strike. He'd come up in the air and down fast with his big old sharp hooves and his mouth wide open. I let go of the hackamore and ran over to the highway and walked up beyond the saloon up the fields a little ways. I walked about two miles and Homer Spencer was coming out of his field on his horse. He'd been down irrigating and I told him what had happened. He said, "Jump on. We'll go uptown and get some horses."

By the time we got uptown and told some of the other boys, and by the time I got my six-shooter, why, all the whittlers were out there on their horses. They all wanted to go back with me to see that horse. Now there was a fellow there we called Highpockets. His name was John Cram. He was six foot six and everyone called him Highpockets. He wasn't known by anything else. And he would bet on anything.

Now when I escaped from that horse and went back to the highway, I thought, "No horse could ever leap that far with a man on him," but it seemed like he'd never light when he did go up in the air. So I went back, made sure I was out of range of that stallion, and stepped it off and it was eighteen feet, you know, just roughly. So I told those guys, I says, "That horse jumped eighteen feet as sure as I'm sitting on this horse." And Highpockets says, "No horse can jump that far," and Gid Findlay, cousin of Eck Findlay who owned the horse, says, "Yes, he can. If Rowl Rider says he can, he can, and here's $100 to say he can." And John Cram pulled out his old deer pouch purse and shelled out $100 in gold, five twenty-dollar gold pieces. Gid matched it and they give the $200 to Jimmy Sorenson to hold. You see, they wouldn't trust each other so they gave the stakes to a neutral party. Then they went over to my brother who was a builder and got one of these fifty-foot tape measures that unrolls. And by that time we had fifty cowboys wanting to see that horse and how far he jumped.

So we marched down there and, sure enough, that horse had jumped twenty feet. And while Eck Findlay shot the horse, so we could get my oufit and, of course, for humane purposes, Highpockets turned over that $100 in gold to Gid Findlay.

Shoeing Little Dickie

This story's funny, I think. I roped a bay, a two-year-old stallion down at Nail's Crossing on the Kanab Gorge on the Kanab Creek.

It was the first mustang I'd ever roped. And he was a fine, deep-chested horse with one white front foot and a white star in his forehead, fine pointed ears and broad between the eyes. I turned him out in the winter range in Nail's Gulch with the rest of our horses for the year and then went and got him in the spring and brought him in. I snubbed him to a cord and he came along with my saddle horse and we went back to Kanab and I put him in the barn with my other horses, fed him grain, and curried the ticks out of his mane and tail. He loved that. I intended to break him, but I didn't want him to buck because I wanted to use him as a cow pony. So I gentled him and learned him to lead and to follow me, and then I put my saddle blanket on him and let him walk around with that. When I decided it was time to get on him, I got my brother, Dave, to snub him for me to the horn of his saddle (on another horse) so that he couldn't buck if he wanted to.

I had a brand-new saddle all engraved and I thought, "Well, I'll go uptown where the boys are setting up there waiting for the stagecoach." They were all sitting on a log whittling. They had three inches of shavings all over the place, and they'd talk about cattle, and about when the railroad was coming to town, and one fellow would say, "Well, if it does come to town, I hope it comes in the daytime so we'll get to see it." And they'd size up new horses in town. And so I had this fine saddle and I was going to be proud setting up on that horse that I had decided to call Dick to show all these cowboy friends of mine a good horse and a good saddle outfit.

Well, I cinched him up all right, got the saddle on–no bucking. I done this without riding him in the corral, just led him around a little. He was used to that. Then I mounted him and my brother snubbed him and we got just about a half a block from my corral going along and, all of a sudden, that little horse let out a squeal and I guess before my brother could do anything, Dick ducked his head down and jerked the rope down off the horn of my brother's saddle and that give him a chance to jump, and we went up in the air. He broke both of the cinches. Dick came down but that saddle and I went in the air no less than fifteen feet. And when I come down again, the ground was soft and sandy, and I went in the ground about a foot. Boy, I thought, that horse can sure go into the air.

Well, Dave said he'd go up to the stockman's store, to Bowman's store, and get a new set of cinches, the front and the rear cinch, double rig it was called, while I held Dick with a hackamore. When he came back, we put the cinches on my saddle and saddled Dick up again, and that time Dave was careful not to let him get his head. So we rode him five, six, or ten miles and came back and then next morning I took him out without a lead horse. And he was very fine, he was gentle, and he was fat. I fed him good. When we got back, Mother called, "Lunch," wanted to know if I wanted lunch before I went on to try him out on the open road. That sounded good, so I put the hackamore reins over the pickets in our front fence on the south side of our home.

We were just about through eating when we heard a tremendous squeal and a crash right at the front door on the south side of our home. Boy, I ran out to the front door and there my horse was hanging up on top of the picket fence with two pickets stuck clear into his stomach. The hackamore rope had come tight just as he was leaping over the fence and it jerked him down and the pickets ran right up into his barrel, right back of his ribs. I held his head and twisted his ears so he wouldn't struggle anymore and Dave took the axe that was right there by the woodpile under a big pear tree and he chopped the pickets down and that let Dick down.

Dave said to me, "Well, go ahead and shoot him," but I said, "Oh, no, I can't shoot that horse." So Dave went to get Isaac Brown. Ike Brown was the only veterinarian and he hadn't had any real professional training, but he did do all the veterinary work in the country there. So we led him down to the barn where Dick's entrails were by now hanging out. We had to tie the horse's hind legs so he couldn't step backward, then we had to pull one foot up and back so we could lay him down without too much trouble. All we had was salt water, hot boiling salt water, for an antiseptic, and so we bathed him in that. And Ike Brown had some needles and some buckskin and he sewed up this hole the pickets had made and we made a canvas sling and bound that around Dick so that the stitches wouldn't be forced open by his intestines. Well, the hole got infected, nevertheless, and in a few days the swelling got so bad Dick couldn't walk forward so he'd back up. He'd back around the corral, back over to the water trough. The veterinarian told me to boil sage and make a good strong sage tea and then bathe him with that every day. Well, I couldn't bathe him standing up because the wound was down in front of his back flank. So I trained him to lay down. All I had to do was lift up one foot and he'd lay down and I'd bathe him and he'd just kind of groan. Well, next then I'd chirp to him and he'd get up. And day after day I'd go down and say, "Lay down, Dick." And he'd lay down. He got so he'd lay down when he saw me coming. It makes me laugh when I think of it now. I would bathe him for half an hour and he seemed to like that. I'd let him lie there and he'd get up anytime he wanted to.

Although he had quite a big welt on his stomach like a hernia, he finally got well so he could travel, so I put him back to the range with the rest of the horses down in Nail Valley. Next spring I went down to get him for the spring roundup. There was twenty of us including W. W. Seegmiller, who run for governor here one time, all down there to round up our horses that had got fat on the winter feed. We all assembled, by prearrangement, of course, at what we called Castle on the west side of the big mountain, Kaibab. Each cowboy had to know how to shoe his own horses and that was his job. We carried shoes in our packs and nails and hammers and clippers so that we could do this operation, because the Kaibab formation where we'd be rounding up our cattle for the next month was rocky and a horse couldn't go barefooted only about one day riding him and his feet would all be tender and you couldn't use him.

I got my other three horses shod all right and I thought I'd shoe Dickie. I called him "Dickie" by now, changed his name to "Dickie" after he got hurt and I had to doctor him every day. He was gentle, but wild, and he was fat, and, oh boy, he came in with the rest of the horses feeling fine. I lifted up one of his front feet, I was going to shoe that first, when immediately he laid down so I just went around and shoed all four feet.

The other cowboys were all hammering away on their horses' feet, you know, the cowboys were all scattered all around this place where there was a nice big spring called Castle Springs. Well, I had one shoe on Dickie before Seegmiller saw me, and then he got the attention of all the other fellows. And they all quit shoeing. They all dropped what they were doing to come over and watch. I got the hind foot shod then, and I rolled Dickie over and he held up his other two feet, and Seegmiller, he laid there, and he laughed till he couldn't stand up and most of the other boys did, too. They all sat down or laid down. But Seegmiller, he just about died. He was about six feet four inches tall and he laid on his back and he'd roll back and forth. He'd roll over there away from me and kinda get a good laugh and then he'd roll back to see me shoeing that horse upside down and start laughing all over again.

Pal

Now we're talking about horses, I'll tell you about another good horse that I had. This was the first palomino horse to be brought into Kanab. He had thrown a cowboy over at the rodeo in Cedar City and jumped on him and killed him. I think the cowboy's name was Bullock. Of course, the cattlemen turned this palomino back on the range. They had all that west range out toward Lund that they turned their horses out on in the wintertime, and summertime too, while they were in the herds with the mares and the colts and that. And then once a year they had a roundup and they'd bring the horses into Cedar City.

So this year, when I was at school there in Cedar City, I'd heard about this palomino horse. He belonged to a fellow named Jones from Enoch, the little town of Enoch north of Cedar. I went down there and this palomino was there and I said, "I'd like to buy that horse," and the guys, some of them said, "Oh, he's a man-killer, you don't want him." And I said, "Oh yes, I do. I want that horse." So they told me this fellow that owned him, and I went over and I made a deal to buy him and I bought him for twenty-five dollars, cheap because he'd killed a man.

And so I borrowed a cowboy's rope there and walked out in the corral and the horses come rushing by from one end of the corral to the other. I put my loop out and picked out both of that palomino's front feet and set him down and tipped him up. One of the other cowboys, while I held his feet, sat on his head, and then I come over and put my hackamore on him. I took him up to Bishop Corey's barn, where I lived in Cedar City there, and made arrangements for Bishop Corey to feed him. And I bought some grain and I grained him and I raked all of the ticks out of his hide. He was full of ticks, you know. Out on the range they got these wood ticks, all the horses did. I just curried them out of his mane, all over. It was in the spring of the year, see, and he had long hair through the winter that had grown. And his hide was just full of ticks everywhere–boy, under his belly, oh dear, and I scraped all of these out with a curry comb and he just loved that. That gentled him.

But I daresn't ride him, so I just put my saddle blanket on him and then I would lead him around the corral. Bishop Corey would feed him then when I'd get home from school, I'd curry him and lead him around and feed him sugar. He was a real pal. I called him Pal. Then about two months before school was out, I finally got up on his back. I knew he'd killed this man, but I put my saddle on him and walked around there for a week or two without getting on him except to ride him bareback sometimes. But he never made any effort to buck or anything. And then I rode him with my saddle and I'd ride him clear to Enoch and back every night after school when the days got longer. That's about eight miles out, eight miles back, and I'd gallop him out there and gallop him back and curry him down and put him in the barn. Then I trained him a little bit how to rope. All the time I'd be riding him, I'd be swinging my rope and dragging it so he'd get used to it. I trained him to back up and hold the rope tight.

Sketches of horses and buffalo found scattered among the stories are by J. Roman Andrus.

So when school was out, I put my saddle on him and I went from Cedar City right straight up over that mountain, that old sheep trail over there, and I landed in Kanab that night at eleven o'clock, and that's a straight line if you didn't have to go through canyons and over mountains and around hills. That was about ninety miles straight through on an airline. And I rode him in one day. He was a dandy horse. Every cowboy I talked to said they couldn't ride half that far in one day over those mountains from Kanab to Cedar City on one horse. And that horse went in on a gallop over that last twenty miles of sand between Mt. Carmel and Kanab.

Next day I got on him and I rode him uptown and went over to my girl's home. Her dad was Frank Hamblin and he was one of the biggest cattlemen in the country. I went over there to just show Pal off, you know. I knew Frank would like him because he was a cattleman and liked horses. He said, "I'll give you $250 for him. Take off your saddle." And I said, "I'm sorry you made me that offer." So the next day he saw me downtown and he said, "I'd give you $300 today for that horse. I want him." And I said, "Boy, I'm sorry again." I says, "I wish you hadn't of made me that offer."

Well, I fussed around with him and I done a little roping there in the corral and branded a calf or two. I've got pictures of him holding a calf down. But one night, by gosh, he laid down in the field down there and there was a sandy place where the water ran out of the main ditch onto the alfalfa, kind of a little shallow place there, and he rolled in that like horses do. They roll in the sand, you know, and then get up and shake. And danged if he didn't roll in there on his back and died. He couldn't get up. He just smothered to death there. I don't know how long he'd laid there until he died, but the next morning he was dead. And I always say it was because Frank Hamblin offered me $300 for him.

Isn't that a heck of a story?

Indian Trading

I'll tell you another story that happened the next year. I was at Cedar City. I went down to the horse roundup again at the same corrals and I spotted a stallion that was about two-and-one-half years old, or at least two, a sorrel stallion and he looked like he'd make a good saddle horse. And so I found out who his owner was and gave him twenty-five dollars for him. And, like old Pal, his hide was full of ticks. And it took me two days working after school hours before I could find them all and dig them out. They were all full of blood, you know, and I curried them out of his mane and his tail and I gentled him that way. And I kept him around Bishop Corey's barn and fed him and grained him–he was kind of poor. It had been a hard winter, I guess, on the range and all those ticks, too. That was the worst thing that could happen to an animal was to get ticks and so many of them. I can't believe, to this day, that there could be that many ticks on one animal. I've dug them out of cattle's ears and back of their ears, but I never have seen them out all over a horse like he had them, especially under his stomach and between his legs and his fetlocks where he couldn't rub them out on a tree or a post.

Well, I fattened him up and trained him every day, learned him to lead good. But I didn't have my saddle in Cedar, so another friend that was to school with me, went with one of the girls from Kanab there whose name was Hicks, and she said her brother was coming with a white-top to take her home and I could ride with them home. I thought that was a good opportunity. So I led this horse home, tied to the back of the white-top. It took us one day to Toquer, the next day to Cane Beds, and the next day we made Kanab. Took us three days to get to Kanab in this white-top.

Nevertheless, I had this stallion down to my barn there in Kanab and I hadn't ridden him yet. I'd been on him bareback but that was all. He was getting fat and was slick and nice. Well, the Navajos came to town and they were making jewelry and trading blankets right up in town, right near the main corner of town right in the middle of the street. So I went down to the barn and got this horse and got on him. First time he'd been out of the corral with me on him. I just had a rope hackamore on him, looped over his nose.

And so I rode him bareback uptown, right up into the middle of the Navajos and got off from him and crossed my arms. One Navajo came out with a blanket, a nice big blanket, and I kept my arms crossed and he threw on another blanket, kind of middle-sized blanket and he stood back there, wanted to trade and I didn't trade. And he looked the horse over again. All these other Navajos came and looked too. They saw he was a stallion and they talked to themselves. And the first one went over and got another blanket off the pile and threw it down and I uncrossed my arms and he got up on that horse like I had been and the horse threw him sky-high. The ground was soft there, too, it was sandy. He came down and all the Navajos they just had a ball, they just laughed and hollered and clapped. Oh, they had the best time, you know, because he went high in the air. The Indian was riding him bareback, but that stallion just went wild. He just really went up in the air and he give about two squeals and on the second jump the Navajo kept on going.

And I thought the Navajo would want to trade back. I supposed he'd want his blankets back, but he just come over and laughed and laughed and laughed. And he says, "Heap bueno horse."

I took the blankets, carried them home. It was all I could do to get home with them. And that big blanket was on our front room floor down in Kanab. It was a tremendous thing about twelve, fourteen feet long and I can't recall just how wide. And it was a beautiful design, a beautiful rug, all red and black and white. A beautiful thing.

Governor George Dern, who was the governor of the state of Utah, came to town and wanted to buy a Navajo blanket, I guess, and somebody told him that if he wanted any blankets he'd better go down to my home and talk to me. He came down there and he says, "I've got to have this blanket." And I said, "Oh, that's not for sale, Governor Dern, I'm sorry you want that." But I said, "I've got these others. Wouldn't you be satisfied?" He said, "No, I've got to have this for my home." I says, "No, I can't let you."

He was going to leave town the next day. Next morning he was back down there. He says, "I've got to have that blanket. I'll give you $350." And I said, "That's twice as much as it's worth, but if you're that set on getting it," I says, "I'll be happy if you'll give me $300." So he took the blanket and paid me. And the horse that I traded for it was only worth twenty-five dollars, that's all I give for him and a bushel basket full of ticks, wood ticks, you know, that was in his hide. And I'd trained him a little bit and learned him to lead and had been on his back, but never had ridden him with a saddle.

And that's the story of the second horse I bought in Cedar City. Isn't that funny? And the other two blankets I still have, and the saddle blanket, the last of the three he piled on before I uncrossed my arms, is out in the Thunderbird right now where we put our suitcases.

Fighting Stallions

I'm going to tell you a story about an act in the animal kingdom that no one in my acquaintance has ever seen.

In the area of northern Arizona and southern Utah, there's millions of acres of land that were used for grazing purposes only by sheepmen and cattlemen. And, naturally, in such a great area there developed, finally, through the years, many wild herds of horses. Some areas yet they still exist and men, in order to preserve the range crop for cattle and sheep, have gone out and shot these wild mustangs, as they are called. But I believe that I am the only man that I ever heard of say that they have ever seen one stallion kill another and take his string of mares.

I was traveling from Kanab in about the year 1908 and as I went on the Navajo trail from Kanab across the north end of the Kaibab Plateau into the House Rock Valley, I came upon two large bands of mustangs, wild horses. They were grazing in the center of White Sage Flat which has very choice food for cattle and also for wild horses. These two bands of horses were lined up in two rows facing each other. On the north side was a black stallion with twenty mares, and on the south side with about twenty-five mares and colts and yearlings, was a white stallion. These two stallions were fighting and their various groups were spectators as intent as spectators in a ball game, one side on one side of the stadium and the other on the opposite side, keeping their distance apart in this battle to the death. In the background, several hundred yards away, were several two-year-old stallions that had been whipped out from the herd by the large stallions who owned the mares and colts so they wouldn't get involved in the fighting.

The white and black stallions reared and struck and bit and they stood on their hind legs and struck with their large, sharp hooves, trying each one to outdo the other. Finally, after maybe ten minutes more, the black horse, after having a front leg broken, was overcome by the white stallion who got him just in front of the withers with his teeth and broke the bones of his neck. Then the white stallion threw him to the ground and just stood and pawed and jumped on him, just cut him all to pieces. There wasn't much left of his body; his hide was all torn, he was all bloody. As I approached, I could see the blood all over the coat of the white mustang, too. He had become red, almost, from the blood of his enemy.

As soon as the black horse quit struggling, this one white mustang, that was the victor, rounded up the twenty head of mares and colts that belonged to the vanquished mustang and run them over into his herd. When he saw me coming he come out to meet me, but before he come to meet me, he started all the horses up toward the mountains. He rounded them up and put them all in one big herd and run along back of them and got them going into a gallop and then he turned around and come back to see me again. And when I got close to him, he turned and hightailed it off into the forest.

This is the only event like this that I have ever seen. I have seen two horses fight each other a little bit, but never have I seen two mustangs fight to the death.[3]

Old Mose Indian

This is a story about the commotion that took place in a little wickiup village in the confines of the city of Kanab, and at this time I happened to be marshal, and I was supposed to keep peace. Two Piute papooses ran frantically and got me and they says, "Oh, come quick, Marshal. Heap trouble down to our village."

So I ran with them down to the creek bottom where they was camped and when I got there there was quite a ruckus. Old Mose had married his brother's wife, which is permissable in the Piute tribe. After the brother dies, he can take over the responsibility of his brother's family. Therefore, he married this other squaw.

---

[3]Rider says, "More than a year after this incident, I came upon the white stallion and his large band of mustangs. This incident I refer to in 'The Seven Bags of Gold.' "

But his first squaw was over in Moccasin, twenty miles from there, and she heard about this. And so in the evening, she got over to Kanab on her pony and she created quite a bit of trouble down in this little village with the tepees down there. Therefore, these two papooses was very desirous that I get there in a hurry.

And when I heard what the trouble was I said, "Pronto." When I got there I said, "Mose, the white man's law won't permit you to have two wives. You, therefore, will have to send either this squaw or that squaw back to Moccasin or I'll put you in the hoosegow."

And Mose then said to me, "Me no tellum, you tellum, Marshal."

Indian Medicine

Well, now, this puts us back a few years prior to the time when the last chief of the Piutes in that area, old Quagance, died. He had got ill, had pneumonia, and they put him in the hospital. But Doc Farrel said he was doing fine and would have been back with his tribe in just a few days.

However, two nights after he went in the hospital, some Indians stole him. I know this personally because his son, Alec, that I rode with a great deal said, "When Dr. Farrel was asleep we stole Quagance and we took him over to Two-Mile on horseback." Two-Mile was the location of a spring and is about seven miles away and they have a subkiva over there. I've only seen one other like it and that's down the Canyon De Chelly. A subkiva's a pit built of stone, arched up and covered with stone. And outside of it there's a great fire bed and they build a big fire and then put stones in the fire and get them hot and then they put them in this kiva and put the patient on top of blankets, wet Navajo blankets. And so they shoved Quagance in there and closed it up. This made lots of steam, of course. And that was the cure for sick Indians.

And I said, "Why did you do this, Alec?" And he said, "White man medicine no good."

"Well," I said, "when you put him in the kiva did the Indian medicine work?" And he said, "Yes, him die."

Butch Cassidy's Escape

I knew Butch Cassidy's brother, Bill Parker,[4] and Bill Parker told me that when the sheriff got the drop on Butch when he went to visit his home in Circle Valley, Cassidy said, "I'll come with you, sheriff, but just give me a chance to kiss my mother goodbye." Her picture was hanging on the wall across the room and the sheriff said, "Go ahead." So Cassidy went over there and acted like he was going to kiss that picture and he put his hand around back of the picture and got his six-shooter and had the drop on the sheriff–and he got away. Took the sheriff's gun. They never caught him.

Of Cowboys and Weather

There's a lot of things that people don't know about cowboys. They don't know that cowboys can tell the weather by their boots. You know, when there's low and high pressure, your boots tell your feet. You can tell by the way they act on your feet whether it's going to storm–rain or snow. Cowboys can always tell that except me. I can tell the day after the storm.

Ten Requirements to Become a "Top-Notch Cowboy"

To become a good cowboy in certain areas, there's ten rules that you've got to comply with before you get your silver spurs.

1. Handle a lariat correctly on foot or on horseback.
2. Rope an unbroken horse within the corral and break it to lead.
3. Saddle a horse correctly. Also, properly set and cinch a pack saddle. See, after a horse is saddled, after you've pulled it up and

[4]Rider rode with Bill Parker–Parker told this story to Rider one time when they rode together from Kanab to Fredonia. Parker also told Rider that Butch Cassidy at that time was in Mexico.

shaped it up nice and straight, you should take hold of the horse's hackamore rope or his bridle reins and walk him a little ways before mounting him. Then he won't buck. And then, after you've ridden him for ten or fifteen minutes, you have to reach down and tighten both of the cinches; you have a little trigger belt, quick setting. You don't have to get off, but you have to tighten it in case you're going to ride or you're going to jump logs or you're going to rope.

And after that, you have to know how to guide a horse with one hand and also to guide him with your knees, nudge him, tell him what to do with your knees. And you've got to know how to hold the reins in your hands, which way to hold them and how to handle them, on the neck with your left hand, swinging from side to side.

4. Properly pack an animal including throwing the diamond hitch. This means cinching, in the shape of a diamond, the ends of the rope that holds the pack saddle.

5. How to approach a horse or a mule to hobble it. This is the "psychological approach" without which it would take two cowboys to hobble the string of horses. Most interesting. It isn't easy. You have to have a certain method. You walk up to a horse with your head down and your hobbles in your hand. You don't look him in the eye. You just walk up and crouch and go down and put the hobbles on him and step back. And if you don't walk up to him like that, you never could catch him. But as long as you go like that, go down, you're all right.

And if the horses are out where they're feeding, then you have to take the rope off their necks and hobble them. See they've got a hobble on their neck. And you've got to know how to put that rope on their fetlocks, and wind it around and slip it through the knot. You just duck your head and go right through their feet and then when you get a hold of their leg, reach up and take the hobble off their neck. And the same way when you go to unhobble them. It's a funny thing. You don't even look at their eyes. You just go down, right towards their feet, just kinda stoop and go right down there on a kind of an angle. And they stand just as still—well, that's a knack. But a stranger couldn't get near those horses if he didn't know how because they just would whirl on him, you know, they wouldn't stand for it. But if you know how to do it, you can do it every time with no trouble. You can't train every horse. But mostly you can. It takes a little while.

6. Memorize the local brands of the area and their position on the animal. Also know the "ear mark" for each brand.[5]

7. Know and be able to perform the proper procedure to rope and stretch out an animal for branding and marking. You've got to catch the calf and you've got to put the de-awelta[6] on and set your horse down and hold that calf and then you've got to get off of your horse and go down the rope to the calf, see, and talk to your horse all the time you're going down there so he won't come forward. Say "Back, back, back." Make him back and hold that rope tight when you're out there wrestling with the calf, see, and you've got to keep that rope tight and the horse knows it. It don't take him long.

8. How to use a "branding ring"–the proper temperature and method. To use a branding ring, you run two wooden sticks from either side through the branding ring, intersecting in an X. The ring is made of iron, flattened, three inches in diameter, and about one inch thick, leaving a hole in the middle about an inch and a half in diameter. Then using the sticks as a handle, run the ring along the hide of the animal, forming the brand. The ring doesn't turn, it just slides along the skin. You have to run the ring slowly over the skin so it will burn out all the hair, leaving a scar.

You have to heat the ring several times unless it is a simple brand like X̂ then one heating will do it. Usually we'd use green sticks or sagebrush so they wouldn't burn, but occasionally the sticks would burn and we'd need to change them. The hotter the ring, of course, the faster you can make the brand; it should be a good cherry red, and that's about as hot as you can get it in a brush fire.

9. Proper identification of cow and calf to insure proper ownership before branding. You let the mother cow search out the calf in the herd, and the calf will follow by her side. See, all the cows and calves are all mixed up and milling around before you brand them, and you need to make sure the calves are part of your herd.

10. To ride a cutting horse without "pulling leather" after the rider has indicated to the horse which animal is to be cut from the retained herd. The horse must be given free rein. For the test you

---

[5]See the story on cattle brands.

[6]A Spanish word which describes the method of winding the lariat around the horn of the saddle.

must cut out ten calves. This is the most difficult test and most interesting to watch. This is to go into that herd and indicate to your horse which critter you want to cut out of that herd and after you've showed him, by his ears he shows you he knows which one you're after as you go through the herd. He spots him, he's got to spot the critter. You slacken the reins, and you've got to let him take that critter out of the herd to the boys on the outside and take it on away. And you can't pull leather; you can't touch leather nor spurs. And that's the difficult one–you've got to ride that horse without pulling leather or spurring. And that horse will take him out of there, boy, and you've got to be a good rider. If you can stay on there, on a good cut horse, you're a dang good cowboy. See, that calf wants to stay with his mother, see, and after you get him out towards the outside, he'll break back into the herd and all of them will try to get back in. And then you've got to take them to the outside cowboys and they give them a shoo back towards the range where they come from. These men on the outside hit their chaps with their ropes and give those cows a jump and a run and they head out back to where we picked them up on the range. And that's the last rule.

Yes, that's quite a job, passing those ten rules before you can get your silver spurs. But at least you don't have to know how to break a horse. The breaking of a horse was up to the professional broncobusters.

And I could do all of those when I was seventeen. Ride and rope–I could rope anything, stretch them out. I could go down the rope and take a yearling, tip him over my hip, put him down. Didn't have to drag out his hind feet. I could go down the rope and tip the calf up. I've gone down and taken and roped those buffalo calves and they're twice as wiry as domestic calves. Boy, I'll tell you, it's something to do it. I've only done that twice, gone down the rope and tipped one of those bawling buffaloes over my hip. Wow.

Cattle Brands on the Arizona Strip and in Kane County

In the little town of Kanab, four miles from the Arizona Strip, most of the men were cattlemen or sheepmen, but the cattlemen distinguished themselves by their brand and their earmark to identify their stock on the range. There were quite a number of cattlemen, so naturally, each man had to have a brand, and I'll recall for you some of the famous brands which were known in that country.

In 1870 Brigham Young called a work mission to build the Windsor Castle at Pipe Springs, Arizona. This castle was built around the spring of delicious water that comes out of the point there and from this point the great cattle range projected to the south and to the east and also to the west, which was like a grainfield. Therefore, Brigham Young organized the Windsor Cattle Company. This cattle company belonged to the L.D.S. Church, but Brigham Young also had private interest in it and the brand was W **W**. In later years, when the federal government took over the Church-controlled property on account of polygamy, it was thought advisable by the Church leaders to put all their property in the names of private individuals so it couldn't be confiscated by the government. And therefore, this W brand became John W. Young's brand, which is JWY. And by the addition of the J on the end of the first V of the W and the straight mark to form the Y on the second V of the W, or **JWY**, this brand was changed and continued to be in active service for many years and later became the horse brand of the Church. And in 1907 and 1908 I actually ran this brand on the left side of horses' rear right thighs to identify them with their owners, the **Z̄** at that time.

Another interesting brand at that time was SOB for Samuel O. Bennion and to the saintly, this brand, of course, would recall the words of Titus when he said that to the pure, all things are pure, but to the unholy, nothing is pure.

Another brand was an umbrella, just a V turned upside down with a dash from its apex down a little below the slopes of the sides **↑**. The man who was identified by this brand was called Umbrella. It's difficult for me now, so many years have gone by, but I believe his name was Palmer. And as far as you could see on the range, you could see that black umbrella up in the air above his horse long before you could see his horse and as he approached other cowboys, their horses were always shying away from him because they were frightened of this umbrella. Really, I think they were giving him the "horse laugh" for carrying it. Nevertheless, my brother, who was one of the large stock owners in the country, was named David Rider and his brand was Bar DR, **D̄R̄**, and one day he and

I were fencing a horse pasture and we were setting cedar posts, which are the best wood for fencing posts, and Umbrella aproached us and he looked down from under his umbrella on top of that tall horse and he said, "Bar DR, I'm ashamed of you." And Bar DR answered and said, "Why, Umbrella?" and Umbrella said, "You know better than setting those cedar posts without charring them first." And Bar DR said, "How come?" Umbrella said, "Because if you char them they'll last you fifty years; I've tried them twice." So I've laughed at that statement. I laughed at the time and I've laughed sixty-five years since until June 4, 1970, when my granddaughter and my grandson were with me on a trip to Jacob's Pools for another purpose (to photograph the pools and the dike that retained the water at the pools—for another story). And that day I had my photograph taken at the cedar posts set sometime before 1915 and I took my hat off then and decided that I would not laugh anymore at Umbrella, because he probably was over a hundred years old when he give us this advice from the top of his horse, shaded by his umbrella. I think he looked like he was over a hundred then.

But there was other brands as interesting, too. One man, who settled at Paria Creek at the little old town of Paria down below Canonville on the Paria River, was named Porter and his brand was Y with an upside down Y next to it, Y⅄ . And we called that the Lord's Prayer, and the reason was that everytime we called at Porter's ranch in the morning to go out to ride the range, he was either getting down to pray or getting up from prayer.

And another interesting brand was the Pratt brothers' brand at Fredonia, Arizona. These men were cattle owners together. And their brand was one of the lazy brands that was used. For instance, an H as you regularly mark it, would be just H, a quarter circle above it as Jacob Hamblin's brand Ĥ and that brand has come down to his sons and to his grandsons now, but when that brand was laid horizontal, it became lazy and we called that the Lazy H I . And so this brand of the Pratt brothers was a figure two lying down horizontally, then the two P's were burned into the cowhide back to back, see, so we called that the Two Lazy Two P ~ꟼP. But whenever we addressed either one of the Pratt brothers, who were big husky men, we just called them Two Lazy, we didn't put on the other two letters.

Some other brands were: the brand of John Findlay, X Diamond X XX. This became quite an estate and still is administered as an estate to the present. FDR recalls one of our late presidents of the United States, but belonged to Franklin D. Richards, one of the early apostles of the L.D.S. Church FDR. He didn't have too much, mostly in Cache Valley. G.A.S. GAS that's George A. Smith; that one would look better on a neon sign up one hundred and fifty feet above a gas station. And Bar JR JR for John Rider was my father's brand. We had quite a few cattle. We ran Bar DR and Bar JR together and they were all over this mountain. E. D. Wooley, who was president of the Kanab Stake for a long while before he died, his brand was DE, just DE, DE and they'd call him Uncle De, see. And he had cattle all over these plains. When I was going down there, Quarter Circle X X, the brand of the Robbers Roost gang, hadn't been run for fifteen years. But W. W. Seegmiller roped a big steer with this brand on it, fifteen years after that steer was branded. They live a long while. He was a big one. Seegmiller always talked about that, roping that big steer.

Well, an Arizona corporation, headed by Stevenson, bought the JWY, the Church holdings, all of them. Called themselves the Grand Canyon Cattle company and their brand was Bar Z Z. Dimmick was their local forman and they employed my brother as straw boss. He did all the cattle work. And by agreement with them, we ran Bar JR and Bar DR with Bar Z.

And then later, when the Forest Service come in here, we had to take them off. Well, the Forest Service restricted their numbers, made us buy a permit, pay a grazing fee.[7] And then there was a drought and everybody lost their shirt; cattle died by the hundreds. Cattle went up canyons where water was and the drought had dried up the water and they'd never get out, they'd just stay there and die. Two weeks, no food, you know. Scarcity of water in the country; everybody had the water rights all sewed up. Well, we drifted our cattle. We gathered them all on the west side of the mountain and

[7]Rider later explained that part of the reason for this grazing fee was that the Forest Service went to a large expense to build a drift fence to separate the local, Kanab, cattlemen from the Bar Z. This ran from Two-Mile to Swamp Point. (However, the Bar Z built a fence from the ledge above Upper Pools, across House Rock Valley, to the Box Canyon at the North Canyon, a distance of about twenty miles.)

drifted them from the mouth of Jacob's Canyon clear across to the Nipple country and then from there down to the Baldies. The Nipple country was our summer range and the Wahweap was the winter range (down where the Wahweap Marina on Lake Powell is now).

The Bar Z sold and moved all their cattle off of here about the same time we moved. They wouldn't pay the grazing fee that the Forest Service imposed on them. They drifted to Arizona through House Rock, across Lee's Ferry, to New Mexico where they had a range. That was the end of the Bar Z.

But my brother still had a big herd. He died suddenly, though, and then his wife sold the remnant to the Kanab people there and then the Church took that over, Kanab Stake, and they've got a big cattle ranch down on the old cattle ranch.[8]

Well, I've run a lot of brands in my life. We put them on the left thigh down on the hind leg. A lot were stencil brands on the end of irons made by blacksmiths and you just heat them. But if you got the cattle on the range, you'd use what we called a branding ring. Every cowboy had one tied to his saddle or had one in his saddle pockets. And this was a ring about four inches in diameter, one-quarter inch thick, with a two-inch hole in the middle. You'd take two green sticks or sagebrush, anything, and run them through the hot ring and you could run the brand, you'd run it around in circles. This is the way I branded those JWY horses, with a little ring. And it would take quite a little while to do it; the cattle or horses would have to be stretched out.

Oh, and then the earmark identified them as well. We put them on one or both, usually both ears. An earmark was the slitting or cutting away of part of the ear either on the upper part or the lower part or the end—some of them were cropped. The Bar Z earmark was a figure "7" and Bar DR was the downfall. That meant the lower part of the ear was slit to the head—that meant the lower part of the ear fell downward; that was why it was called a downfall. And looking at cattle, you could always tell a Bar DR or Bar JR cow. Bar DR's right ear fell downward, and Bar JR's left ear fell downward.

---

[8]Rider added that LeRoy Wooley (the last baby born in Windsor Castle when the U.S. marshals were looking for polygamists) took over Kane Ranch which had been Bar Z's winter headquarters. He ran it until he died, in the spring of 1973.

And these brands and the earmarks that went with them, of course, were recorded in the county's record and they would hold up in court against cattle rustling or cattle-brand changing which often took place. Of course, cattle or horse rustling was a serious crime at this particular time in Arizona, punishable by hanging. But most people were honest. Mavericks, you know, are unbranded cattle who have been weaned from their mother and, regardless of age, if they do not have a brand or an earmark, they become anyone's property who can catch and brand them. But in order to make sure that the critter did not belong to any other cowman, it was the practice to just earmark it first and then later, when it was found on the range, if no one else had claimed it, then to rope it and put on the brand. This I have done quite a few times myself. And so that's a little story, a very minute story, of the history of brands in the Arizona Strip and of the Kane County cattlemen.[9]

Songs of the Range

The following are "songs I was requested to sing by the cowboys as we sat around the campfire after a long day's work. If my brother, Dave, was present, he would accompany on the harmonica." *Rider records the following as being the setting for these songs: the cowboys would be sitting around a campfire and they could* "hear in the silent night the hooting of an owl, the crying of coyotes and if you listened carefully, you would hear the listing of the wind in the forest.

"One of the most popular songs that I was asked to sing around the campfire for the other cowboys, when we rested after a hard day's ride on the range, was 'Sweethearts.' I'm not sure where I learned that but my dad used to sing to me a lot when I was a kid and I learned a lot. He was a good singer. I don't know why I remembered the words. And Alex, an Indian, with whom I rode as a companion on the range, always requested 'Falling Leaf.' I think as I sing it you will understand why he made that request. But it wasn't very often we could get together and have a campfire songfest. Everyone was tired and went to bed."

---

[9]Rider stated that cowboys made one dollar a day, thirty dollars a month, "and foremen, like my brother Dave, made $50 a month and board."

I asked him whether other cowboys used to sing, too. "Oh, sometimes they would hum along but I don't remember any that could sing. Sometimes they joined in with a little tenor. But what I sang were all love and romance songs."

"*Did you have any cowboy songs?*"

" 'Run Along Little Dogie,' but I never liked that song. Some of the boys riding along the side would sing it while driving the calves along."

Sweethearts

A little maiden with eyes of laughing blue,
Cheeks with sweet smiles laiden,
Hair of golden hue;
Standing in the Moonlight, bowed her curly head;
Jack, our dream is over and tonight we part she said.

Chorus:

> We were sweethearts, Bess and I,
> Dreaming of happiness in the years gone by,
> Loving and trusting, thru weal and woe,
> Until there came a parting–we were sweethearts long ago.

Cross words were spoken,
Bitter words were said,
Cherished vows were broken–
All our love was dead.

Chorus:

You may go your way–I will go mine,
You with another, true happiness will find:
The past will have no sorrow or disappointment
When you forget we ever met and will never meet again.

Chorus:

Time has its changes and there came a day
When I met a woman, oh! so feeble, old and grey.
Kind Sir, she faltered, won't you please help me;
I am an outcast and in poverty.

Chorus:

Tears dimmed her faded eyes, her head bent low;
I knew her then, we had met again,
We were sweethearts long ago.

Chorus:

Falling Leaf

Far beyond the rolling prairie
Where a noble forest lies,
Dwelled the fairest Indian Maiden
Ever seen by mortal eyes;
For her smile was like the sunbeam,
Daughter of an Indian Chief,
Came to bless their home in Autumn
And they called her Falling Leaf.

Chorus:
    Falling Leaf the breezes whisper
    At thy spirit's early flight;
    From within the lonely Wigwam
    Comes a wail of woe tonight.

To this land of Laughing Water
All alone one wintry day,
Came a hunter, lost and weary,
On his long and lonely way.
Days passed by and still he lingered,
Gentle Falling Leaf he cried,
'Til with a kiss of love she promised
Soon to be his woodland bride.

Chorus:

One bright day this hunter wandered
O'er the forest trails alone,
Long she watched and long she waited,
But his fate will ne'er be known:
With the Summer days she faded,
With the Autumn leaves she died,

Then she closed her eyes forever
By the roaring river's side.

Face in the Fire Light[10]

I sat by the fire on the hearth stone,
The embers were burning low,
And scenes of the past came before me
And pictures of long ago.

Chorus:
  Only a face in the fire light,
  Pictured within my heart,
  Pleading with me from the embers
  Asking why we should part;
  Only a face in the fire light,
  A dream of a winter's night.

I scarce said goodnight to the old folks
Who stole softly off to bed,
For there was this face in the fire light,
The face of a love long dead.

In 1967, after Rider had finished singing this song to a group of his workers at his plant, the Rider Plastic Company, one of the men recorded Rider's comments.

"Not a sound would be spoken after I finished this song, not a word of thanks. All the men gazed into the fire light probably seeing the faces in the flickering fire light and remembering events that had taken place in their lives. Some were young and some were middle-aged men, all rugged in their characters and in their aspirations in life.

"Nevertheless the silence was only broken by the wily, spine-chilling yell of the coyote in the distance or the hoot of the hoot owl in the nearby pine or by the listing of the wind in the forest, which, if one will take time out to listen to, he will hear. It isn't obvious but

---

[10]Of this song, Rider stated: "Every cowboy loved this song and usually would steal off to their bedrolls. When I camped alone–I often sang this song to keep the coyotes company."

it's a sound of nature and referred to in the Bible, 'where the wind cometh and goeth, no man knoweth, where it listeth, no man knoweth.'

"The men then would, one by one, seek out their bedrolls, protected from the elements by the tarpaulin. (In those days, before the bandaid or the tent, we had no facilities for carrying a tent and we never knew what a bandaid was.)

"So this is a memory that has come back to me over sixty years and I'm happy to record this. I want to close with the thought that the God-given mind of man is more wonderful than all the electronics of the modern age."

Part Two

Of Guns, Gold and Near Starvation

Seven Bags of Gold

Since, in my early youth, I was a cowboy eager for the thrills associated with wild mustangs, the lariat, wild, renegade long ears, and bawling, pouncing calves—campfire stories during these years found me an eager listener. I heard at first hand about lost men in the forest who, according to these stories, never traveled in a straight line but wandered about on the arc of a circle. This behavior of rational men seemed rather unreal as I had never had the experience of being lost. The stories also told of lost persons who, instead of getting panicky when they knew for sure that they were lost, gave their horse his head and were brought safely into camp. They often swore that they felt the horse was traveling in the wrong direction all the time.

The natural instinct of direction seems to be inherent with the animal kingdom, but in man this instinct has to be developed. One's environment must be carefully studied by constant vigilance day and night; one must note the direction of winds, the bending of flowers, the shadows, the moss on the bark of trees, the difference and density of foliage on hillsides, the direction of drainage in all draws and ravines, and many other natural signs. It also requires a constant observation of our universe night after night; the position of all the visible planets and prominent constellations in the heavens every month of the year must be known.

On one occasion, my three companions decided I was leading them in the wrong direction in the forest and under the stress of being frantic, none of them could identify Polaris. Being overruled three to one, I told them I would follow them until they decided they were going in the wrong direction. Half an hour later we walked into the low burning embers of the campfire we had left shortly after dark. This experience proved to me that men actually travel in a circle when losing their sense of direction. I have had other similar experiences to this one but believe this is sufficient for the purpose of this story.

In the fall of 1909, I was camped at Jacob's Lake, Kaibab Forest, Arizona. I was a lonely cowboy sitting on my bedroll watching the slowly dying embers of my campfire. Occasionally the ring of the bell on my pack mule or the yelping howl of the coyotes nearby would distract me from the faces I thought I could picture in the flickering firelight. Suddenly I became conscious of a different noise and strained my ears to get a more-distinct sound and, though it was very low at first, it became louder and I could determine the rhythm of unfaltering footsteps of an approaching animal. In the silence of the forest about me, I could determine it was coming directly toward my campfire and I watched with anticipation because from its direct approach I knew it must be a friendly visitor. I threw onto the dying embers some pitch splinters and a bright flame lighted the darkness about me. At the same moment, two long ears and the bright eyes of a pack mule came between two big pine trees. Immediately behind him a trudging, tired stranger shouted, "Hello!" I invited him to throw down his pack while I prepared him a late supper, and boy, was he hungry. He hardly said a word until he had eaten everything I had prepared.

The next morning, after breakfast, he inquired the direction to House Rock Valley and Lee's Ferry. As I was waiting for a runner with instructions from the foreman of the Bar Z outfit and since I had nothing in particular to do, I rode with him for a mile on the trail and outlined the directions for the rest of his journey before I returned to my camp.

Night came and no runner appeared and again I was watching the dying embers of my campfire and dreaming of happier, less lonesome nights, and again the rhythmic thud of hoof beats descended upon my ears. They approached directly toward my fire and I stood up to welcome the runner I had waited so many days for. And, just as I threw more wood on the dying coals and the fire lighted up the darkness, the bray of a tired mule broke the silence of the forest and between the same two big pines sauntered the weary pack mule and behind him the old prospector, visitors of the night before. It was just sunup when I bade him goodbye that morning on the trail to House Rock Valley, and now, according to the stars, it was almost midnight. He had traveled in a complete circle without stopping and had come into my camp from the same direction he had come to my camp the night before. Upon recognizing me, his first words were, "How in the world did you get away out here?"

In the darkness it was rather difficult to prove to him that I was in the same place that I was when he came to my camp the night before. It was necessary to take him to a small, covered well on the edge of the lake in order to really convince him. I remember the expression on his face when he finally realized that he had traveled all day and part of the night and arrived at the identical spot he had left so early that morning. This to me was an unusual event because the prospector was driving a mule supposedly in the direction he thought was right, but the mule gradually deviated just enough from that course to finally come to the place where he could get relief from his pack and get water and forage. The prospector did not know he was lost and had no occasion to panic while he was traveling which probably would have cost him his life. It was for this reason that it was so difficult for him to believe his mule had completely reversed his direction of travel without his master knowing it. I prepared supper for him again.

The following morning, I told the prospector I would go far enough to put him into Trail Canyon from which point a definite trail could be followed to his destination. As we started our journey, the sun was well up and I took lead at a slow gait, carefully watching the mule tracks in the grass. At a distance of about five miles from camp, the mule tracks turned gradually from the general eastward direction in the forest but I continued straight east toward the head of Trail Canyon. At this point I bade the prospector goodbye and good luck. He thanked me many times and expressed himself as being most grateful for my help and hospitality and, after traveling a short distance down the trail, turned and said, "I am most thankful that my mule has a great deal of horse sense."

I supposed that he would find his way to House Rock Valley and Lee's Ferry without further difficulty and I would not see him again. He told me he came from Nevada but did not tell me his name. This was my first experience with a genuine prospector who had all his provisions and equipment on his mule and yet had no animal for himself to ride.

It was a glorious ride back through the forest, bunches of deer leaping away into the quaking aspens and occasionally the unusual white-tailed squirrels ran from pine to pine or sat up watching me as I passed.[11]

[11]The white-tailed squirrel is one of Rider's favorite animals. On our trip to the Kaibab we spent at least forty-five minutes chasing one and trying to get his picture. Rider explains, "The Kaibab Forest is the only habitat of this beautiful tosseled-eared and white-tailed squirrel. They climb high in the pines and leap or partly fly downward to the branch of the next tree, but if they are frightened will climb to the topmost point of the tallest tree."

That evening the runner I had been expecting came with instructions from the Bar Z foreman that I was to go to the Paria Ranch and drive twenty-five head of pure-bred Hereford yearling bulls to House Rock Valley. These bulls had been shipped from Iowa to Marysvale, Utah, the nearest railroad terminal, and had been drifted in short stages from Marysvale to the Paria Ranch. My instructions said to be most careful in handling these animals as they were worth more than $2,000 each. My mission was an important one as I would be cowherd to the first "imported" bulls into the Kaibab territory. Several days later I, my faithful horse, and pack mule, after traveling through many miles of country I had never before seen, came upon the Paria Ranch. The large grove of cottonwood trees, under which I could see a small cabin with surrounding cultivated fields, was a beautiful, welcome sight to me. I was greeted at the gate near the cabin by Mr. Porter, who gave me the welcome news that supper was just ready.

The next day, while my saddle horse and pack mule were enjoying a much-needed rest, I inspected each of the bulls carefully to see if, in my judgment, it could withstand the long five-day trek to House

Rock in the House Rock Valley. There were twenty-three head I felt could make the journey. Sunup of the next day found me started on the trail with my twenty-three head of valuable bulls. My thoughts turned to the hospitality and home-cooked meals of Mr. and Mrs. Porter and I turned in my saddle a number of times to wave goodbye as they stood under the great cottonwood trees. It had been more than a year since I had seen a woman or eaten meals prepared by one. This visit aroused in my mind many happy experiences of home and loved ones. These thoughts kept resounding in my memory as I hazed my charges slowly southward along the trail toward my destination. My pack mule took the lead and my horse, trained in the ways of handling cattle, weaved back and forth, patiently nudging the trailing bulls. In my experience with drifting cattle, there was always, no matter how small or how large the herd, one who always was in front and led the way and there were also many trailers which had to be prodded forward. The leader of this group I nicknamed Curley Top. My pack mule would gain some distance ahead and then would stop to graze until Curley Top reached him and then he would jaunt forward again. He used this method each day and since he had been trained to follow a trail, never did he deviate more than a few yards to either side to forage.

Soon after sundown, I arrived at the first day's destination which was Rattlesnake Springs. My charges were thirsty and so were my pack mule and my horse. After tanking up on pure spring water and replenishing my canteens, I moved out some distance from the spring in order to obtain better forage before I threw pack for the night. May I say here that a cowboy's life in this section of Arizona began at daylight and finished at sundown or later without a stop for lunch. This held true too for the saddle horse and pack mule.

Usually cattle on the trail had to be guarded at night to keep them from scattering in all directions, but my bulls had been raised together in pastures and at daylight the next morning I found them grazing peacefully. They were grazing in the same direction with Curley Top on lead. The same procedure as outlined for the first day and night continued the next four days of the journey. We stopped at Buckskin Gap the second night, at Coyote Spring the third, at Two-Mile, the old Indian battleground, the fourth night, and arrived at my destination at House Rock Valley the fifth night with twenty-three sore-footed bulls following old Curley Top. I was happy to have fulfilled this part of my instructions without having lost any of the animals enroute.

I was now on the Bar Z winter range and the grass was stirrup high and I knew that the bulls would survive in their new range. My instructions were to wait at House Rock until one of the straw bosses came down from the winter range on the Kaibab. I had no idea when this would be but I was to help him in gathering semi-wild saddle horses ranging far south in House Rock Valley along the rim of Marble Canyon. This I knew would be an exciting experience and would take every ounce of skill of both riders and their mounts to gather and force these horses from their native range. I looked forward to this experience because it offered excitement and adventure and would compensate for the long, lonesome trek with Curley Top and his twenty-two followers.

The arrival of my friend, Archie Swapp, the straw boss from the Bar Z outfit, was a happy occasion for me as I loved to have company. At sunrise the next morning we mounted strong, fast horses and by sundown had rounded up this herd of horses and, after many exciting moments, brought them into the great spreading wings leading to the corrals and water tanks at House Rock. The water at this point was piped eight miles from springs at Two-Mile and was padlocked during the spring and summer seasons. This protected the winter range from all grazing and provided grass and browse for the Bar Z cattle that grazed on the Kaibab Forest during the spring and summer months.

The intructions Mr. Swapp brought me stated that I was to help him with his horses up the Kaibab and through the drift fence into Trail Canyon, and, after this was done, I was to go with an important sealed letter to a Mr. Emett at Lee's Ferry.[12] One unusual and

---

[12]Rider explains, "The ranch at Lee's Ferry, owned and operated by Jim Emett, was isolated in either direction by more than ninety miles of ungraded road from the nearest towns. Mr. Emett, by virtue of controlling the water, thereby controlled the cattle range in the area. He had built up a considerable number of cattle and quite a sizable herd of horses which grazed the year round on his domain." Mr. Rider further explains, "All public domain, except that under the Forest Service, was dominated by men or companies who controlled the watering places which were relatively few in the area of House Rock Valley. All cattle that grazed in these controlled areas were considered strays by the outfits who owned the water and were drifted out by them. The Bar Z outfit owned all the water in House Rock Valley, except Emett Spring and Soap and Badger Creeks, all of which were in the eastern part of the valley and bounded on the north by the Great Vermillion Cliffs and

interesting episode, which occurred while riding at a gallop behind wild horses after we got them into Trail Canyon, was that I exchanged shirts with Mr. Swapp since he was going to town and did not wish to be seen in his ragged and torn and soiled shirt. Bidding him farewell and hoping he would find his sweetheart loyal and true, I turned back to House Rock and to another lonesome but interesting trip into a new and foreboding territory.

I looked forward for the coming daylight the following morning and anticipated the new adventure which would take me along the trail I had almost three weeks before directed my prospector friend. I expected to follow his footprints to Jacob's Pools, then to Soap Creek, the next watering place, then to Badger Creek and from there to Lee's Ferry, a total of more than forty miles which I hoped to cover by sundown. It was in the fall of the year and the grass in House Rock Valley waved in the breeze like fields of grain in Kansas. The day was hot and when I arrived at Soap Creek, I threw my pack and saddle to give my horse and mule a half an hour rest while I rested in the shade of a pinnacle boulder which is common at this creek crossing. Also, I wondered what had happened to the prospector whose footprints I had followed to within two miles of my present location. They had turned off to the right of the trail and I had expected to find them at the creek crossing as there was no other place a man and a mule or even a man could proceed toward Lee's Ferry. As I leaned on my saddle I was pondering what could have happened to my friend and as I gazed across the plain toward the direction the tracks had led, I thought surely he had come to a tragic end. I determined, since my mission was urgent, to pursue those tracks upon my return.

I continued on to the Ferry and arrived about sundown and partook of the hospitality of Jim Emett, his wife, two sons, and eight daughters, and above all I enjoyed fresh fruits from the orchard and delicious watermelon from the fields. Reluctantly, I left the ferry at sunup the next morning for the return trip back to Kane Ranch, thirty miles south of House Rock but on a different route. I carried a sealed message which was to be delivered to the foreman of the Bar

---

another barrier, the Marble Canyon, on the southeast. These two barriers converged at Lee's Ferry. This point thus was the only feasible crossing of the Colorado River between Moab, Utah, and Harper's Ferry, Nevada, four hundred miles downstream."

Z outfit. I learned later the reason I had been the emissary to Mr. Emett was because of the ill feeling and hatred that existed between the Bar Z outfit and the Emett spread, and because I was just a very young man whose father and brother, Dave, were friends of Jim Emett. As I wound along the trail of the Colorado River, my thoughts occasionally turned back to the Emett family and especially to the youngest and most beautiful daughter, but more often to the delicious fruit she had given me that morning.

I arrived at Soap Creek and watered and refreshed my animals and myself and made my stay short because I wanted to settle my curiosity about the old prospector. When I arrived at the point on the trail, I followed the foot tracks to the south across a rather shallow canyon, and when I reached a higher elevation, from which point I could see a good deal of the rim of Marble Canyon, to my surprise, there in the distance, near the rim of the canyon, was the prospector's mule and I concluded that if the mule was still alive after these many days that his master also must be and was carrying water to him. I reined my horse and wheeled about, happy in my thoughts that the prospector was continuing his vocation. My mind turned then to the long hard ride to Kane Ranch.

I arrived at Kane, the winter headquarters of the Bar Z outfit, and I was happy in the thought that I could replenish my food supply and get some badly needed clothing. I arrived at about sundown and was greeted at the hitching rail in front of the cabin by Mr. Dimmick, the Bar Z foreman, who had come down from VT Park, the summer headquarters, to receive the sealed document which I carried from Jim Emett. This man was, in my estimation, very reserved and quiet and until he opened the document which I took from my pack I had never seen him smile. We prepared supper together after which he said, "At last we get rid of the long thorn in our side. Jim Emett has accepted our offer to buy him out lock, stock, and barrel." We talked late and he outlined the part I was to play in the transfer of all the Emett cattle, horses and material to be left at the Lee's Ferry Ranch. My intructions were written out in detail.

Mr. Dimmick left for VT Park at sunup the next morning and I shod my three fresh horses and another pack mule which Mr. Dimmick had brought down from the mountain. These horses were to play an important part in the transfer of the Emett stock at House Rock which was the agreed delivery point. I was to be the only Bar

Z cowboy present at this delivery. However, the agreement with Mr. Emett was that Bishop Henderson, from Cannonville, was to receive and tally all stock according to the classifications stipulated in the proposal by Bar Z.

I was thrilled with my new assignment as I knew that there would be much excitement and much hard work involved. I was to go to House Rock and check all corrals, the water tank and the eight-mile pipeline to its source and check the horse pasture fence and other incidental details relative to the delivery which was set approximately two weeks from that date.

One night, while awaiting the coming event, I was sitting by my campfire, a lonesome cowboy dreaming of the luscious watermelons and the beautiful cowgirl at Lee's Ferry and wondering if she would be there when I again returned. The yelping howl of coyotes broke the silence of the night and I listened to see how long it would be before all the coyotes in the nearby area would join the chorus. A stranger not familiar with these animals would swear that there were at least 100 of them in the chorus, but as each howl joined the initial one, I could spot the direction and I was sure there was not more than five. As the chorus died down, I heard the familiar rhythmic hoof beats of an approaching animal. I threw on my dying fire some cedar wood and stood in front of the blaze, facing the approaching footsteps. As my eyes became accustomed to the darkness, I made out the form of a pack animal and, just as I did so, the familiar bray of a mule greeted me and again my old prospector friend shouted, "Cowboy!"

I helped my friend with his pack, watered the mule at the corral and took him over to the horse pasture. I returned to my camp and prepared a meal for a hungry and weary traveler. This time he was more talkative and after he had finished eating, he took from his alforjas[13] seven small, canvas durham bags and said to me, "Hold out your hands." He put one at a time in my hands and I thought from their weight that they surely must be filled with lead. He took them and placed them on his tarpaulin near the fire and said, "Would you like to see what is inside?" He untied each one of them, then very

[13](Rider pronounces it au fo gay) Heavy duck bags or wooden frames covered with leather with leather strap loops–looped over the pack saddle horns.

carefully opened wide and I looked with amazement as I beheld seven bags of glittering gold.[14]

Buying Out Emett (Or, Looking Down the Barrel of a Six-Shooter)

This following's a story I've never told before; I'd made a promise at gunpoint not to. In the year 1909, I think I was eighteen years old, in fact I know I was, I was a cowboy riding for the Bar Z Cattle Company, also called the Grand Canyon Cattle Company, which was the biggest cattle company in Arizona. At the time, they had for their cattle range the entire Kaibab Forest and also the great House Rock Valley as their winter range, a domain forty-five miles long and

[14]This story is different from the others in that, although told orally, it wasn't told before an audience but rather was dictated to Rider's wife, Romania Rider, who then transcribed it from shorthand. It was also told quite a bit earlier than the others, about 1956. The style, as a result of it being dictated, is much more studied and formal. This can easily be seen by comparing the ending of this tale and one I taped when we were down in the area and Rider was casually telling the story to my cousin, Steven Rider, and me. The conclusion of that recounting, all that was recorded, is quoted below.

"I was sitting around my campfire out there in front of that old rock house, just going to kick it out or let it simmer out, and go to bed, and here come this "tromp, tromp, tromp," you know, again, and I looked up and here was the old mule and the prospector come right into my camp again at House Rock. So I got him something to eat and I said, "I thought you was going to Lee's Ferry," and he said, "Oh, I got sidetracked." And I said, "Yes, I know that, I saw your mule down on the point." I guess he might have told me how he watered him, but I don't know. I said, "Where'd you go from there?" and he said, "Oh, I went down on the Colorado River." So after I got him something to eat here it was bedtime again, maybe ten o'clock at night. Coyotes a-howling through the valley there. Now that was the third meal I'd fed him.

"And so after we'd eaten, we were laying down there and he said, "Do you want to see something pretty classy?" and I said, "Yes." He got over there in his alforjas and he had seven little sacks filled with gold. Of course, I didn't know it was gold and he just handed me one of them and gad, my hands went down and mashed my knuckles on the ground. That gold was heavy. You know, he just handed me that bag, he dropped it in my hand, whop, my golly. Then he opened one of them and showed me and he got seven bags of gold in three weeks down there; somewhere down there where Soap Creek goes into the Colorado.

"So that's the story of the seven bags of gold. I never seen him again, never heard of anyone who did. He come on up the trail then he went on up to Jacob's Lake and went on back to Nevada, or wherever he was from."

forty-five miles wide, triangular, which they jealously preserved, and no outside cattle except my father's and my brother's cattle were allowed on it. And down at Lee's Ferry, which is about sixty miles from the headquarters of the winter range ranch at Kane, on the west side of the House Rock Valley, was another cattle spread originated by a man named Jim Emett who ran the ferry there for the Church of Jesus Christ of Latter-day Saints and also for what profit he could get out of it.[15] Over these years he had built a great herd of cattle but he had no range for them except the House Rock Valley, Bar Z's winter range. He therefore became a thorn in the side of this great cattle company, the Bar Z, who had at least 100,000 head of cattle in that area. Plus it soon became obvious that Emett was stealing cattle from them because, out of a herd of just scrub cows and bulls, that he had taken for toll for crossing the ferry from emigrants who had towed them along with their wagons to furnish food (he would take anything, guns, anything he could get as payment), he had now produced a herd of white-faces that were just about as good and looked about as good and were the same breed as the Bar Z stock. The Bar Z had gone to great expense to import bulls and those bulls probably cost $1,000 apiece time they were got into that area.

It became evident that in order to separate these two herds that they would have to build a drift fence to separate the water rights of Emett, which was Emett Spring, from those of Bar Z. So they built a $30,000 barbed wire fence[16] which ran from the Jurassic fault scarp,

[15]James Emett ran Lee's Ferry in 1895 after his predecessor, Warren M. Johnson, had become incapacitated. And "on November 8, 1896, Warren and Permelia Johnson sold their interest for $6,500 to Wilford Woodruff, trustee for the Church of Jesus Christ of Latter-day Saints. The deed conveyed about thirty-two acres of lucerne, six acres of orchards, vineyards and garden and one-and-a-half miles of ditch." Arizona, Coconino County, Recorder, Deeds, Book 4, p. 228. P. T. Reilly in "Warren Marshall Johnson, Forgotten Saint," *Utah Historical Quarterly,* 39 (1971): 21, records that "Dee Wooley had recommended James S. Emett to succeed the injured ferryman and Johnson acquired Emett's promising Cottonwood Ranch in the complex deal."

[16]In another account Rider speaks of the difficulty they had in building this fence. He states, "They had to haul that wire from Marysvale down here. And then they had to get the posts over here on the Kaibab, snake them down the hills there you know, with horses and chains, and load them and carry them over here and build a fence here. Took quite a crew of men. Most of them were Tropic men and Cannonville men they hired from up there."

a ledge on the north side of House Rock Valley which forms a natural barrier that only birds can get over, to the North Canyon barrier which ran near the Lower Pools, which was the last water right of the Grand Canyon Cattle Company. This seven- or eight-mile fence would prohibit the Emett cattle from coming in and eating up the winter range of the Bar Z Company, whose cattle were always drifted onto the high Kaibab Mountains through the spring and summer months and into the fall.

But occasionally after this fence was built, we would still find herds of Emett's cattle grazing over on the Bar Z range and we would investigate and we would find that Emett and his sons—he had two boys and eight girls that were just as good riders as boys—they would stampede this buffalo herd that was in that area (it consisted of about 150 buffalo) and they would stampede them and tear this fence down for eight or ten rods. And then that next day, of course, here would come all of Emett's cattle, grazing on the Bar Z winter range. It would take ten or twelve cowboys and the fence repairmen about two days to search out all the valleys and canyons to get the cattle back beyond the fence and repair the fence again. Plus Emett would increase his herd by twenty-five or thirty cattle at a time by shooting the mothers and stealing their calves; some of those cows that he killed had twins, you know. I can take you to one box canyon where there's twenty-five skulls still remaining probably today. Emett could make a herd pretty fast when he'd get twenty or thirty calves at a time, you know. I'm not saying he shot the mothers, but they've got a bullet hole in the middle of their skulls.

So, as a result of all this, the Bar Z and the Emetts were bitter enemies. They carried guns. Dimmick, the foreman of the Grand Canyon Cattle Company, always carried a six-shooter on his belt, was never without it, and so did Emett and his two sons. And they swore that they would kill each other if they ever came in close enough range.

Emett had been taken to Flagstaff by virtue of the Bar Z hiring a detective cowboy to check on Emett and he had been subpoenaed and was in court at two different occasions at Flag. But both times the jury acquitted him because of lack of sufficient evidence. If they could have found the evidence though, Emett would have gone to the gallows because a man got the death penalty in the state of Arizona for stealing horses or cattle. It was the only way the cattlemen could protect themselves.

Now this man Emett was quite a character. He stood six foot four and I tell you he had steel gray eyes. He'd look right through you. I know this because I had to look at him a time or two. He was the master of that entire range for hundreds of miles because on account of the barriers no other cattlemen could get in there. He was right down in the neck of a bottle and no one could get him out. He was there to stay. And that's the way he built up his great herd. And then in the fall of the year, he would take his steers, swim them across the Colorado River, and take them over through Tuba City and into Flagstaff to sell them. So this war became more bitter year by year and the Bar Z tried to buy him out.

And I was the man, I was a young cowboy, that was the only one in the group that dared go down to Lee's Ferry, down in the Emett domain. I've never seen any Bar Z men go in that area at all. No one would ever go beyond the pools. That drift fence, that was it. They'd go and repair the fence but they never saw any of Emett's people. But I wasn't afraid of Emett. He had been a friend of my brother Dave's. In fact, Dave had lent him his horse, Ned, to ride in a rodeo in Kanab in the fall of 1907.[17] Emett didn't win, even though he was a fine horseman and an expert roper, but it was the first time he'd ridden Ned. So I knew Emett from that. We were friends.

Well, now, I went down on various occasions with my horse and pack to take negotiations to Emett from the Bar Z headquarters. The time of the sale was set, the price was stipulated—so much for calves, so much for cows and calves, so much for two- and three-year-old steers, so much for mares and colts, so much for geldings, so much for stallions—all was specified in this contract price. Now these terms, each of them had to be okay'd by Emett, and then I would have to take his proposition back to headquarters at Kane for Dimmick, the foreman, and Stevenson, who was one of the main owners of the company, to figure out whether they would accept or need to

---

[17]I wondered how Emett could ride so openly in a rodeo in Kanab in 1907 if he was a "wanted" man in 1909 and presumably for a few years before then, so I asked Rider about this. Rider said that only the Bar Z men were after Emett. No one in Kanab was concerned. So Emett came across the range during the night, by way of Buckskin, to avoid the Bar Z men.

make a counteroffer to this man Emett who had cost them so many thousands of dollars for quite a number of years.

Finally, after several months, the terms were agreed on, but the cattle and horses still had to be delivered to House Rock Ranch which is under the Kaibab on the western slope of the winter range in the House Rock Valley. They had great corrals there and water tanks which were filled by water piped by Bar Z for about eight miles from a spring at Two-Mile up in the sandhills. And there, at House Rock Ranch, the cattle were to be branded from the Emett brand into the Bar Z brand. And a man by the name of Bishop Henderson, a fine man from Cannonville, Utah, was the neutral man chosen by both sides to transfer these cattle and Emett and the Bar Z took his word. Henderson kept a tally of all the calves, all the cows and every critter that was branded and turned. And he marked this in his record and on this record it showed the price that the Bar Z had to pay Emett.

All of these cattle, by the way, were delivered by Indians. None of the Emett family, not even the girls or boys or Mr. Emett himself, approached the Bar Z territory at all. They never came beyond that fence I was telling you about earlier, the drift fence we called it. Emett's hired Indians rounded up the cattle and brought them into the corrals there and corralled them, then they would leave and go back and gather more cattle. And then they'd get the horses the same way. And they cleared out all of the Emett stock entirely exept for one stallion which they couldn't get.[18] I helped brand all these cattle. I helped brand them and change their earmarks and so forth. And then, of course, this whole valley, this great House Rock Valley, after this transaction, this became the Bar Z range because Bar Z then owned all the water in that valley.[19]

On the last day, when all of the cattle had been turned over to the Bar Z Cattle Company, I was instructed to go to the headquarters at Kane and I rode to Kane and there I received from Steven-

[18]This is the subject of a later narrative.

[19]As a postscript later in this account Rider states "By virtue of owning water, the law stipulated that you also owned the range rights. But, since that time, the Taylor Grazing Act has changed this. Now on all the ranges all over the country, they're divided up now so that nobody, although they own the water, can actually own the land around it."

son, the president of the Board of Directors of the Grand Canyon Cattle Company, written instructions fulfilling the terms of the contract which had already been entered into between them and this man Jim Emett. It stipulated in there that I was to pay Emett, after measuring the hay that he had on his ranch, so much a ton for that hay. I knew how to measure hay and to do that. And I had to pay him so much for every dogie calf he had there and for every old milk cow that had not been drifted to the House Rock Valley, which was sixty miles away up to the House Rock Ranch itself, and there were other stipulations there. It was necessary for me to fill out the blank check signed by Stevenson after I had done this work.

I started on my way and after awhile I approached Soap Creek which was twenty-five miles from Lee's Ferry.[20] A little trickle of water comes down there across from the red ledges to the north and if you dig in the sand, water collects there and you can water your horses. And that's the way the cattle would water; they'd water in the tracks that they'd made in the sand–it was the only place the water would collect as there was not enough water to form a stream. So, as I approached this place, I took the saddle off my horse and the alforjas off my pack horse, so that the animals could rest a little while and the blankets dry, and I laid in the shade of one of these umbrella rocks that are prevalent down there in that particular area and especially right there where the trail crosses Soap Creek. And I figured that I would do the next twenty-five miles late that afternoon and get into Lee's Ferry about sundown. And as I was laying in the shade of this big umbrella rock, I noticed two ravens and they were flying around a little hole in the rocks up on the ledges about a quarter of a mile away. And I watched them and watched them and couldn't figure out what it was all about. So I went toward this ledge and near the base I picked up big boot tracks. I was really curious now, so I clumb up the ledge, the last little slope was kind of hard climbing, but I got to this little pocket that was about as high as I could reach, and in the pocket I found two ears with a seven on each ear–that was the Bar Z earmark–and a square foot of hide with a Bar Z on it. That was the brand on the hide. The ears

[20]The highway distance between Lee's Ferry and Soap Creek is 14.5 miles. Certainly, however, the old horse trails were not as direct, and the distance that Rider actually traveled could have been close to twenty-five miles.

and the brand were stuck behind a rock about eight inches by four inches which was wedged in the pocket.[21]

Well, I couldn't figure out where the carcass was, so I went back down to the creek where the seep crossed the trail and I saw there some offal out of the paunch of a cow and I knew I was on the right track. And so I followed down this little seep and then down where it dropped off about twenty-five, thirty feet, I saw down in the gorge the carcass, or the rest of the hide and the legs of this critter, who now I had the ears and the brand of.

So I laid there until almost dark, deciding whether to go back to Kane or whether to go on to Lee's Ferry because this was the evidence that twice before they had needed to convict Emett for stealing cattle. It was ironic that the final day that they were to turn these cattle over, Emett went from his spring and went to Soap Creek. Cattle were always in there to water and he, or one of his men or children, killed one of the Bar Z critters, although he would be paid soon for all the cattle that he had turned. So it was up to me, just a kid, to decide whether or not to take this evidence to Stevenson, the owner of the Bar Z Cattle Company at Kane—which would have cancelled the deal and probably sent Emett to the gallows—or to go on down to Lee's Ferry and say nothing about it. After several hours I decided since Bar Z had bought Emett out and since he was moving out of the country and the deal had already been made, I'd go on to the ferry.

So I went on to Emett's ranch at Lee's Ferry and I got there late at night. I took my horse over by the shed and unsaddled him and unpacked my pack horse. I just had got a little campfire started to going and was getting my frying pan out, and as I was doing this Mr. Emett came out and he says, "Anything I can get you from the house?" And I said to him, I said, "Mr. Emett, have you any fresh meat?" And in the flash of a second I was looking down the barrel of that big six-shooter and I didn't like the looks of it. He says, "What do you know about fresh meat?" And I says, "I don't know anything." And he says, "Oh, yes, you do." He knew that I had to

---

[21]In June 1970 my cousin Steven Rider and I followed Rider's instructions and easily found this "pocket" exactly as he described it. Inside the pocket was the eight-by-four-inch rock, wedged in there exactly as Rider said. (He said he replaced it the same way he had found it.)

come by Soap Creek where he killed that cow, see, and he thought I must have seen that evidence, that carcass. But I really hadn't meant anything by my remark.

I finally said, "Yes, I have the ears and I have the brand but I haven't got them with me. I buried them over there at Soap Creek and I decided after two or three hours I'd come and forget the thing." But he said, "Well, I haven't forgot it."

I'd already ridden forty-five miles that day, but he said to his son, Dude, to saddle up a certain horse for me to ride and to saddle his horse, and Dude did. He put my saddle on one of their horses and I rode, then, for twenty-five miles in front of that man with the six-shooter back to Soap Creek. Of course, this was all riding at night and I didn't know any minute whether he was going to shoot me or not, but I didn't think he would until I uncovered the evidence, so I was pretty happy about that. I would have felt better, though, if he would have talked to me. I kept feeling he was determining what to do with my body after he had recovered the evidence I was going to dig up for him. I used one statement over and over. "Mr. Emett, the fact that I did not return to Stevenson and Dimmick at Kane Ranch should surely convince you that I'm your friend." I also said, "You're my brother's friend and this fact helped me make up my mind to go on to the ferry. And I have, after my former visits to your home, felt a great deal of friendliness and sympathy for your family who have been so kind to me." But not one word did he answer in reply. I recall that my prayer was that he would realize that I had done what was right in his behalf—the last five miles of the trip I left the decision in his hands.

We got to Soap Creek and I dug up the brand and the ears. Then I didn't know what to do. And I was pretty frightened. It was a pretty precarious position for me as a kid. My thought was that he'd drop me in the Colorado River where the road paralleled the stream near the ferry. The river flowed into a box canyon there and he could've kicked me off and no one would have ever known what happened. I don't know what he would've done with my horse and pack, though.

"Well," he said finally, "Come on. I'll tell you my story." We rode side by side then along this trail. It was kind of an old wagon road there, very, very rarely used, wide enough, though, for horses to go side by side along most places. Anyway, we rode side by side and he unfolded his life story since he had been there at Lee's Ferry from 1895 until 1909. He was a pretty good talker. I think now he was trying to get my sympathy, but I didn't think of that then. It was quite a story–I hadn't known anything about these things. He told me about his family and he told me about the two times they had taken him to Flagstaff to this court, how he'd been acquitted and so forth, and how he met Zane Grey at the second trial and took him in.[22] He told so many things, about hiring teachers and building a little schoolhouse there at the ferry and how he'd paid out of his own money for teachers to come there every year and teach his eight children.[23] And, of course, that was one thing the defense attorneys in Flagstaff talked about, what a great man Emett was, to think that he would hire someone and take them out there, ninety miles from Flagstaff, to teach his children in that Godforsaken country.

Well, we passed the point where the road went near the river without incident, so, by the time we were nearing Lee's Ferry, I was feeling pretty comfortable and I said to Mr. Emett, "You know, Mr. Emett, this would make a dandy story to tell Zane Grey." Emett whirled around and said, "Now listen, and listen good. I've spared your life but you are never to tell what events transpired here while I'm alive. I want you to promise to that." I was certainly in no position not to, the advantages to the story not being told were mutual. I should have turned Emett in, and more than one cattleman would have been upset that I hadn't.

We arrived back at Lee's Ferry and after we'd measured the hay and counted the cows and I'd made out the check for him, it was for $65,000 plus whatever the hay was worth, I've forgot, then I helped him load the wagons and I saw a whole wagon bed full of Navajo blankets for which Emett had traded the Navajo Indians there on the Navajo reservation; the Indians would swim their horses across the river and trade with Emett. And the other trinkets he had mostly was bedding and probably one or two items that he wanted to take out of there. The rest of it he couldn't haul because there was no

---

[22]This is the subject of a later narrative.

[23]In 1971 Rider contacted David Leigh in Cedar City, Utah. Leigh's wife, Julia, one of Emett's daughters, had died, but Leigh related that he was one of the schoolteachers Emett had hired and that while at Lee's Ferry he had fallen in love with Julia and had married her.

road. He had four horses on one wagon and two on another, and he had a scraper tied on the back on one of them because they had to make a road to get out of that country. And so I got quite well acquainted with the family in the two days I was there helping him gather up his things, and when they rode out, I rode the twenty-five miles back to Soap Creek with them.

I kind of took a shine to that little girl called Lena, one of Emett's youngest daughters, same age as I was.[24] And she could ride, boy, she could ride. She could go along with a rope and run her horse through it and everything else and just wonderful. So we rode side by side then all this distance, or until we got within about five miles of Soap Creek, and then Emett come back on his horse and he said, "I want to talk to you a minute." And he sent Lena on, told her to go on and we'd catch up. So he and I rode along together. Now he offered me at least $500, I can't remember exactly how much, but to me it was a lot of money. But I says, "No," I says, "I don't want any money." I said, "The reason I didn't turn you in was because I thought you were moving out of the country and you'd had enough trouble down here in this country as it is." I knew some of the things that had happened.

Then he said, "If you won't take any money, here, take my spurs. They're my pride." They were silver mounted, made by the Navajos, and all inlaid with silver. The straps over the top had solid-silver conchos on them. The buckles and everything were inlaid. And even the rowels on the spurs were inlaid. And they had little silver bells that hung down from the spurs so you had this little tinkling of the bells as you rode your horse along. Boy, they were beauties. I couldn't believe he gave them to me.

And so we parted. I shook hands with the whole outfit. They all stopped and I waved my old cowboy hat and told them goodbye and I turned back to Lee's Ferry to await further orders from Bar Z.[25]

---

[24]Lena, we learned from her husband, Samuel Bennett of Holden, Utah, died in the fall of 1969.

[25]The Arizona, Coconino County, Recorder, Deeds, Book 355, pp. 285–86 records that "The Church of Jesus Christ of Latter-day Saints and James S. Emett sold the ranch and the ferry to the Grand Canyon Cattle Company on August 18, 1909, and September 11, 1909."

Further documentation of the history of the management of the ferry is given on a plaque erected by the Daughters of Utah Pioneers, No. 350, on the site of the fort at Lee's

Enter Zane Grey

Zane Grey entered into the picture during the trial of Jim Emett by the Bar Z Cattle Company[26] which I mentioned previously. And Emett told me Grey had come from Ohio. His father had sent him from Ohio with a letter and $500 in cash to an old fraternity pal of his from the university who was now the presiding judge in Flagstaff, Arizona, and who presided at this trial of Jim Emett. And Zane Grey's father said in this letter, "The doctors here say that my son, Zane, has tuberculosis and won't last, only probably three months, maybe not that long, and if you will take care of him, or find some ranch out there that will take care of him until he dies, and bury him, you can have the $500. I've sent all the cash I could dig up with him, outside of his train fare, and if you'll see that this is done, I'll appreciate it very much." And that was the extent of the letter.

So Zane had got there about two days before this trial and he was still living at the home of the judge. And the judge, by virtue of Zane being a guest in the house, got him a seat in the courtroom which was a very difficult thing to do because it was a notorious trial and all the cattlemen from all over the country came in there. They even built scaffolds up all around that courthouse on the outside to watch these proceedings through three big windows there.

Well, now, because this was the second time Emett had been brought in, they thought surely they'd get a conviction this time. That's what all the cattlemen were wishing, at least. So the judge had a good seat right near the witness stand for Zane during this trial. And after the second day of trial, the jury come in and ac-

---

Ferry. It says, "John D. Lee settled here in December 1871 and established ferry service. Thirteen months later, after her husband's death, Warren M. Johnson ran the oar-driven ferry for Emma Lee, 1870 to 1875 when the Church of Jesus Christ of Latter-day Saints purchased her interest. Johnson served until 1895. He was followed by James S. Emett who sold to the Grand Canyon Cattle Company in 1909. Coconino County operated the ferry from 1910 to 1928."

[26]This is substantiated by Angus M. Woodbury in "A History of Southern Utah and Its National Parks," *Utah Historical Quarterly,* 12 (July–October 1944): 192–93, who says that Zane Grey came to Arizona in April 1907, and that, "Incidentally, Zane Grey built his novel, *Heritage of the Desert,* around Emett's trial at Flagstaff in April, 1907. Emett, whose headquarters were at Lee's Ferry, had been accused of rustling by the B. F. Saunder's [Bar Z] outfit."

quitted Emett. (This was one of the things Jim Emett was telling me on our trip back from Soap Creek to Lee's Ferry that night.) Zane Grey jumped up, shook Emett's hand and he says, "Mr. Emett, I feel like I know you from the evidence that's been brought out here in this trial and the description of Lee's Ferry and so forth." And he said, "I would like to go with you to your ranch. I have $500 and here's the letter that my dad wrote to the judge here and it specifies that you can have this money if you will take care of me until I die and bury me out there." And Jim Emett says, "You're my man."[27]

So Zane Grey then went to Lee's Ferry. The old judge probably hesitated about giving him the okay on this trip, but Zane was determined to go. So that was how Jim Emett met Zane Grey.

And every day then, now I don't know the exact number of days or the number of months, but Emett had Zane sleep out in the open, and every day he sent him up on the mesa to take care of a little band of sheep he had up there. Zane Grey'd go up there and herd those sheep every day and round them up at night and put them in a little corral there so the coyotes couldn't get at them and then he'd walk back down and he gained his health out there in the dry air and sunshine.

And so this was the advent of Zane Grey into Arizona and also into his storytelling because, out of this experience, he became attached to the great outdoors and Arizona and the cowboys and the cowmen that he had met out there.

Incidentally, it was about in 1907, two years before the event I've been telling you about of the Bar Z buying Emett out, that I first met Zane Grey. Now on the occasion that I'm talking about, the foreman of the Bar Z ranch, Dimmick, and I were camped at House Rock Ranch after having made a previous arrangement to meet within a two- or three-day period as there was no communication in the area except by word of mouth. And we were sitting by our small

---

[27]This story was related to Rider by Jim Emett on their return trip from Soap Creek after Rider had dug up the evidence which would have indicted Emett. Rider acknowledges that the account is thus secondhand and possibly subject to error. But perhaps the reason for the vast discrepancy between Emett's account of why Grey was in Arizona and Grey's biographical accounts, which record that Grey came west to gather material for a novel, not because of illness, is that Grey was "playing the part" of his hero in *Heritage of the Desert* who was supposed to be in Arizona for his health.

fire on the saddle porch of the rock house which is close to the corrals that I have spoken of, those tremendous corrals, inside of which was a reservoir and also pine watering tanks.

It was dark and we were just ready to roll into our blankets when the big swinging gate creaked and called our attention to some intruder at the corrals. So I went down immediately toward the corral to see who it might be, as a stranger was welcome because I had been there four or five days alone before Dimmick came. And I wanted to see if it was someone I might know in the country. When I got there it was Jim Emett and Zane Grey. They had had time to water their horses and their packs, each had a pack, and were just coming out of the gate when the foreman of the Bar Z ranch approached. When he saw who it was, of course, he drew his six-shooter and he would have shot Jim Emett had I not kicked the gun out of his hand. I was sixteen years old but I was all muscle and had had good experience in wrestling and boxing, and I held Dimmick so that he couldn't recover his six-shooter. And Emett also carried a six-shooter, but Zane Grey begged him not to shoot Dimmick, the foreman of the Bar Z.

Now the only thing I could say was, "Move on, because I can't hold this man forever." They mounted their horses and drifted. And they were going to meet Uncle Jim Owens with whom Zane Grey[28] hunted lions.[29]

---

[28]Rider's personal comments about Zane Grey are most interesting. He states, "Incidentally, going back to Zane Grey and his hunt with mountain lions on the Kaibab Forest, it has been recorded by some writers that he was a great rider, a great hunter. Well, I can tell you after we had run a lion down, got him treed, killed him and skinned him, then we'd have to take up the hunt for Zane Grey, and have to hunt for him about half a day, because he couldn't keep up with us. He couldn't ride like the rest of the cowhands and he couldn't leap over logs like we had to do to follow the hounds, and, therefore, he'd be lost within about fifteen or twenty minutes in the forest. Zane Grey didn't have the ability nor the training and this is easily understood because he had had no experience whatever in packing and riding which he obtained in later years. But, of course, his stories are fiction, and naturally he'd want to be classed as a real cowhand."

Rider continues, "The men whom he characterized in his first story, *Heritage of the Desert,* were acquaintances he had made while in Arizona, one of whom was my own brother, David Rider, and another one was a good friend of mine, Brig Riggs, and another was a good friend of mine too whom he wrote about later, Eugene Stewart, who trapped wild horses on the Kaibab in baited pens with salt rock. . . .

"I have often said that I would set up half the night telling Zane Grey stories and I didn't know at the time that he was contemplating becoming a millionaire by quoting

The Black Stallion

After the horses had all been turned into the Bar Z, there was one stallion that the Navajos couldn't capture. And he was a black one and he was a beautiful horse. He was up on the mesa above Soap Creek. There's quite a mesa there, runs from there to Lee's Ferry and all of Emett's horses were raised there and they ranged up on this mesa. And this horse was too good for the cowboys. He could outrun any of them and he got away, so they couldn't bring him in to be sold to the Bar Z outfit.

After the cattle and horses had all been turned at House Rock, this one Navajo said to me, he said, "We've got one stallion still out there." He told me to tell Bishop Henderson, who turned the stock,

---

these tales into print. A lot of the stories I told him, more or less, were true to life and true to a cowboy's life and I exaggerated a little occasionally just because I didn't think he knew what I was talking about. . . .

"As soon as I read the obituary of Jim Emett, the wife and I went to California to tell Zane Grey the story of his benefactor and the man who, according to Emett anyway, saved his life, for which I hoped to receive five percent royalty of all sales and all movie rights by so doing. At morning we were instructed from his home in Altadena that he had gone to Australia and so we were disappointed and returned to Salt Lake City and later I was advised that he died after his return from that trip."

Asked about Zane Grey's description, Rider said, "He was blond. Weighed about one hundred sixty pounds. At the time, I weighed one hundred eighty. And he was light complected and when I first met him I realized that he hadn't been in too good a health. That was my impression at least. He didn't seem robust like my companions and cowboys that I knew from day to day and rode with. He had an observing, inquiring mind, though, and he listened intently to anyone with whom he was speaking and I realize now why he became such a good writer and a good descriptive writer. And he also was aware of the beauties of that area of the country, Marble Canyon, the Grand Canyon, and the Kaibab Forest with its thousands of deer. . . . He was too serious-minded to have a sense of humor and this led me to believe that he had a serious illness. Of course, at this time, I did not know the entire story of how he became acquainted with Jim Emett. . . .

"Now why he didn't like the Mormons is something else because two of us were the only Mormons in the outfit that he associated with and I don't even think he knew we were Mormons. Emett was supposed to be a Mormon, but whether or not he was, I'm not sure of that, either. I believe Emett's wife was a Mormon. But he went down to Fredonia to live. And he told some wild stories about that town of free women. That's what Fredonia means. But he didn't know what he was talking about half the time. . . . He was just a young fellow, you know, out in the west for the first time. But when he went down to Fredonia then he got all the history about the Windsor Castle out at Pipe Springs and how all the Mormons kept their polygamist wives out there."

[29]Mountain lions or cougars.

about this horse and wanted to know if they could get money for it. And of course, they couldn't get it. The specifications said only those horses and cattle that are branded can be paid for and so Henderson told the Indian that. And I said to Henderson, "Can I have that horse if I can catch him?" And he says, "You surely can. You're welcome to him."

So I took Alec Indian, who was one of the cowhands, my best Indian friend who I'd ridden with for several years, a very fine roper, and we went to Soap Creek that afternoon and we went up the trail at the head of Soap Creek. And as we got up to the head of Soap Creek, to the spring, we saw fresh track, a fresh sign there that he had just been in to water. We followed his trail out onto the first mesa and sure enough, he was out there on the mesa grazing. He went out on a point and I went ahead of him so he couldn't go around the mesa and Alec come behind him and so we ran him down on this point overlooking the valley below. Well, I went one way around, I went to the left, and Alec come to the right and we knew that that horse would have to come by one of us and we had a chance of roping him. We both had fine horses.

But as we approached the end of the point, there was an island of stone about twelve feet high and extending about a quarter of a mile toward the end of the point, and this stallion was back of that. Neither one of us could see him, but we knew he had to come between that ridge and the edge of the mesa to get by us, and we had the best opportunity there to rope him. But when we got over to the end, he wasn't there and we couldn't imagine where he'd gone. We looked down in the valley–and there was a string of dust going towards Soap Creek. That stallion had leaped from that ledge which is fifty feet, at least, and hit the slope below and had slid down through there. It's a wonder it didn't kill him. He passed Soap Creek and left just a string of dust behind him, running as fast as he could run out into the open valley.

And we never saw any more of him. We went on around and up to the head of Soap Creek and come back down and we thought we'd find him out there somewhere and we kept riding into the sunset, but he turned off toward the left out there. We couldn't track him, of course, but we thought he'd go toward House Rock because the other horses had been drifted that way and we thought he'd take their trail. But when we got to House Rock about dark, he wasn't anywhere in the area. I had to go to Kane the next day and Alec had to help scatter these cattle we'd just bought of Emett's out to the various watering places, some up at Two-Mile up at the old battleground, and some went to the Upper Pools and some were drifted toward Kane so they would be acquainted with the new range and the waterholes and so forth.

Anyway, three weeks later, after all of this transaction had taken place, I was waiting at House Rock for my friend, Archie Swapp (who plays an important role in one of my lightning stories), and I was lying out there with my bedroll, out in front of this old rock house at the House Rock corrals and reservoir there. No one in the country at all, just I alone and I woke up one morning at daylight and down toward the corral about 100 yards from me was this black stallion surrounded by six or seven coyotes all ready to jump on him. His head was almost touching the ground and he looked like just skin and bones, and he was really. That was three weeks that horse had gone without any water and without eating anything.

Well, I jumped up and pulled on my boots. I knew those coyotes were waiting for him to die. Just as I was pulling on my boots, I

looked up and he'd keeled over and those coyotes had jumped on him and tore him open before I could get down there. And so I got my horse, saddled him up, and drug that stallion's body over south a little ways into a little ravine out of the way there, off of the area round the fences that guided the horses and cattle into the corrals. But he didn't weigh anything. He was just skin and bones. He was hurt internally, you see, when he jumped off that ledge, and his hide was all scarred up, his legs were scarred from the injuries coming down off that mesa. And I just left him there. Those coyotes, though, had been watching him for a long while. You know, they were waiting for him to die. And they put up a great hallo that night. Boy, I thought there was 150 of them, but although the whole valley seemed full of coyotes, really there was less than a dozen of them. They'd have had quite a feast of that black stallion.

And that's the end of that beautiful black stallion that no one could catch and Alec Indian and I couldn't either. And rather than be captured with a rope, he jumped off of that ledge. And I could show you that sometime, I can show you that very ledge where he jumped off. You wouldn't think a horse would do it, but he did.

Julius F. Stone Expedition

After Emett had left the ferry, I returned. My instructions were to remain at the ferry until replaced and I didn't know how long that would be but I hoped not too long. I wouldn't sleep near the old dwellings there, John D. Lee's cabin or the old two-story driftwood home that Emett had built for his family. I went out in the orchard a little ways away and threw my bedroll down there.

I was sound asleep one night when I was awakened by voices calling intermittently from the direction of the ferry, about a quarter of a mile from where I was. Now the ferry is hemmed in by tremendous, perpendicular, impassable ledges and by the Colorado River. It would be impossible for anyone to pass through the area without crossing the ferry, which would require my help, or by coming down the river in boats which hadn't been done since Major Powell did it in 1869. So I supposed it was Navajos who had swam their horses across the river. They were coming along the trail toward the ranch and as they drew closer, I decided they were not Indians; I could tell from their conversation they were white men and I could tell they didn't have horses but were walking. I was happy to know they were white men. While I was a friend of the Navajos too, I was glad to see somebody, even though I couldn't figure out how they got there. It was pretty lonesome country.

When they got about within a rod of me, I spoke up and I says, "Hello," and they all ran back up the trail. And they sure went, boy. I says, "Come on back. We're friends, down here." They came back and one of them introduced himself as Julius F. Stone and in turn introduced his three companions. One of their names was Galloway and one was a photographer. I can't remember the other.[30] He informed me that he was from Columbus, Ohio, and that he and his companions were the much advertised Julius F. Stone Expedition going through the Colorado River from Green River, Utah, to Needles, Arizona. And he said, as I knew, that this was the first expedition down the river since the initial successful exploratory expedition of Major Powell. Stone's trip, essentially a picture-taking one, was news to me as I hadn't seen a newspaper for months nor had I seen anyone who had heard of this.

They had run out of food and so I cooked them up what I had, and boy, did they eat. I thought they was going to eat everything my old alforjas held. They said, "Well, we'll have some food for you tomorrow." They wanted to know where the owner or the operator of the ferry was and I said, "No one here but me." And Mr. Stone was quite concerned. But he said, "Well, we'll still find food tomorrow morning." He says, "I have a letter where they're to bury this cache of food in case there's no one here." He handed me a copy of the letter he had sent to Emett. In it Stone outlined the essential foods that they would need to make it possible for the continuation of their trip. He listed all these and enclosed a fifty dollar money order to compensate for the items. Then he underscored the following words: *"In case there's no one at the ferry, make a cache of these articles within a twenty-five foot radius of the north support of the cable that pulls the ferry."* So Stone asked me to meet them there at daybreak and to bring a shovel if I could find one.

Well, I was so excited with the events and the prospects of having company that I couldn't sleep and was glad when the first colors of

[30]Dubendorff.

morning shot up over the red ledges. I pulled on my boots and was successful in finding a broken-handled shovel. I hurried up the river to join Stone and party, who were still asleep there in their sleeping bags. My saddle horse was so excited when he saw the three bright-colored boats that he stampeded and I let out a war whoop. I caused such a commotion that my friends thought the Navajos had found them and they scrambled out of their sleeping bags. They were happy to see it was only me.

As soon as they were dressed, we went up to that ferry mooring, you know, that cable mooring there. And we dug all that day until dark and all the next day until noon. Five of us out there, blisters on all our hands, everyone helped. But we couldn't find that cache. There wasn't one, by the way.[31] By using my food and some powdered milk of Stone's, we prepared some meager meals.

They decided, because of the food situation, they couldn't stay any longer and they asked me how much bacon I had, and how much flour and how much dry fruit. And I had some beans, too, by the way. I didn't have very much. Just one man don't need very much, you know. And so I said they could have all of it except about one pound of flour and a half a pound of salt bacon; I was expecting a relief to come around the ferry, anytime, maybe tomorrow, maybe

---

[31]It is interesting to compare Rider's version with Stone's. "Wednesday, October 27, 1909 . . . We reach Lee's Ferry at 12:35 and go into camp among the willows opposite John D. Lee's stone fort . . . the fort is deserted, as is also the ranch house that was occupied by Mr. Emmett [sic] when we were here before, he having sold out to a cattle company and gone to Kanab, so Mr. Ryder [sic], a cowboy whom we find here, tells us. A careful search for the supplies we were expecting to find in the place where they were to be cached is fruitless. We also ransack the ranch house and corn crib with the same result, except that we find about three pounds of dried apples and half a pound of raisins. Galloway, who knows Emmett [sic] better than I says, 'I believe the old cuss has kept the money and purposely forgot the supplies.' If so, it is very awkward, because we have but three or four pounds of flour, very little coffee, no baking powder, bacon, or anything else. In fact it is an aggravating situation. When I was planning this trip I wrote to Emmett [sic] who then lived here and whom I knew, sending him a check for fifty dollars, with the request that he have ready for us at the time of our probable arrival enough provisions, flour, bacon, one ham, coffee, baking powder, et cetera, for five men for ten days, also in case he should be away to cache the stuff, properly boxed, at the upstream side of the stone fort. This he wrote he would do." Julius F. Stone, *Canyon Country; the Romance of a Drop of Water and a Grain of Sand* (New York: G. P. Putnam's Sons, 1932), pp. 83–84.

Ironically, Rider says that a few days after Stone had left, an Indian came with the supplies. Stone didn't know this until twenty-one years later when Rider and Stone met in Columbus, Ohio, at Rider's instigation and Stone honored him with a banquet.

the next day. I didn't know. Well, nevertheless, I gave them that and they decided to go. They estimated that by doubling their daily traveling hours and with scant rations they would be able to make it.

Mr. Stone, during the time of our searching, had unloaded everything from the three boats and had dried out all the wet equipment and discarded every possible item that he thought would be unnecessary for the hazardous journey through the Grand Canyon. Now they reloaded their boats and every pound of equipment not absolutely necessary was left on shore. About one o'clock, after a scanty meal of rice and bread, they bade me goodbye. They got into their boats and buttoned up around their necks a waterproof jacket which was attached to the boat with fastenings. The boats had been built in Grand Rapids, Michigan, especially for this trip, and contained watertight compartments in either end. They also contained waterproof food compartments.

Mr. Stone manned the first boat, Mr. Galloway the second, the photographer and boatman manned the third boat, and in this order they rowed out into the river and swung their boats into the half-mile rapids. I mounted my gray saddle horse; I had to ride along the bank at quite a trot and a slow gallop sometimes to keep up with them.[32] This was really an experience for me as I expected all of them to be lost before they reached the quiet water at Marble Canyon at the end of the rapids. They were expert boatsmen and kept a distance between them of thirty or forty yards, following the course set by Mr. Stone. I saw each of them disappear in one extra bad spot but they reappeared and soon entered the box canyon at the entrance to the Grand Canyon area.

I had ridden my horse out onto a large flat shelf protruding about a foot above the water level and extending into the center of the river about twenty feet, and was waving and shouting goodbye and good luck, when to my surprise, all three boats swung into the eddy below the projection on which I was and rowed their boats right up to me. They unfastened their jackets and all came out upon the rock with me. They gave up the trip. Stone said he'd decided they

[32]Stone records: "Thursday, October 28, 1909 . . . And so at 1:23 P.M., having had a light lunch, we start. Mr. Ryder [sic] . . . [is] on the bank to see us run the first rapid which we do in a little over four minutes, and at its foot say good-by to Ryder [sic] who has ridden along the bank at a gallop." Ibid., p. 84.

wouldn't go. No mail for them, no nothing there, no food. So I says, "You guys are crazy. You go on down there and you'll find all kinds of food down that canyon." I'd ridden every point all along there and I'd seen a few mountain sheep up high on the Marble Canyon ledges, way up. But I'd never seen anything in the bottom because no one had ever been down there since Powell went through. But I thought they certainly would find something. I was just a kid, you know, I was only eighteen. I've kept the Word of Wisdom all of my life and I've been prompted so many times that saved my life—maybe I was prompted to tell them that they would find food. I don't know. I was just an ordinary cowboy, I didn't know if there was anything but grasshoppers there, if that. But anyway, I says, "You go ahead, Mr. Stone."

After they had shaken hands and left again, I was sure that I was going to be the cause of their death. I hoped that they'd change their minds again and come back, but as they disappeared around a bend, I reluctantly turned back to my camp in the orchard and soaked my blistered hands. My humble prayer to God that night, as I crawled in my blankets and closed my eyes, was that they would make it through the canyon. But I didn't think they would.

I didn't know that their trip had been successful until I got back to Kanab, six or eight months or a year later, where there were letters and a picture he had taken of me waiting there.[33] But ironically enough, it wasn't until twenty-one years later in August, 1930, that I was informed at a banquet given in my honor as the guest of Julius F. Stone in Columbus, Ohio, that my predictions of food for their journey came true. Mr. Stone addressed an audience of 250 men and said, "This cowboy saved our lives by predicting that we would find food down the river. Through an act of Divine Providence, we found five head of domestic sheep about twenty-five miles below Lee's Ferry. We preserved every bit of that meat by drying it and boiling it and making jerky out of it and it supplied us with ample provisions for the balance of the expedition."[34]

---

[33]This picture is the frontispiece of this work.

[34]Stone records that they saw five *goats* on a ledge at Soap Creek, and that they were able to shoot down one and that that goat "ended all prospect of short rations." Stone, *Canyon Country,* p. 85.

But when Stone asked me to talk, then I said, "I don't want to disillusion our good friend, Mr. Stone, but that was not an act of God that those sheep were placed there, but it was an act of the devil really." And then I told them about the range war between the sheepmen and the cattlemen where lots of men were killed in Utah and Wyoming. You see, when sheep graze, cattle will just sniff and stick their heads in the air and drift. They'll drift day and night. They'll never eat a bite. And so the cattlemen were afraid this whole, vast cattle country would become sheep country and they'd lose their herds. Well, the sheepmen decided to trail 10,000 head of sheep across this area and the cattlemen thought they were going to graze them permanently here so they cut the dikes and two reservoirs, Two-Mile Reservoir and Jacob's Pool Reservoir, so these sheep couldn't water. I know who did it but I never told anyone. I might tell you it wasn't me. But this let those 10,000 head of sheep choke from thirst so much that when they smelled the water of the Colorado River, although they were up seven hundred and forty feet from it, on those ridges there above where Stone navigated those rapids, all 10,000 plunged over to get water. Every single one of them went over the brink. The herders couldn't stop them. They just piled up, dammed the river. And I've seen the bleaching bones on the first shelf which is about forty feet down. And they filled that up and then they bounced off of those and went right on down to the river seven hundred feet below.[35] But five of those domestic sheep drifted down twenty-five feet to Soap Creek where Stone killed them.

---

[35]Rider states that on the ride back from Soap Creek (see story "Buying Out Emett"), "Emett told me about all this, and he showed me right where they [the sheep] left the herders and went." Emett also said, according to Rider, that "his daughters, after this had happened, took a rowboat and rowed down to where they [the sheep] went over the brink. And they skinned for several days until the stench prohibited them from continuing any more for several days. And they rowed those pelts back up in the rowboat to Lee's Ferry. And they sold them to Navajos, no other outlet, you know, traded them for blankets, or for jewelry. That's all they had; the Navajos had no money. Emett's daughters had some wonderful rings and bracelets clear up to here on their arms, that they traded for those skins. The Navajos, of course, they took the wool off and wove it into rugs and they preserved their hides to make leather clothing and sandals and so forth." Samuel Bennett, who married Lena Emett, the youngest daughter, said Lena often spoke of this incident when we talked to him in Holden, Utah, in 1970.

Gee, those guys at that banquet they all stood up. They wouldn't believe such a thing could have been possible, but it's the truth. That's a great story.

So that's the final episode of my contact with Julius F. Stone and his expedition down the Grand Canyon at the time I told him it was the act of the devil instead of the Lord that provided him with food to make that trip.

Part Three

Capers on the Kaibab

Scaring President Roosevelt

One of the greatest experiences of my life was making the acquaintance of our great President of the United States, Teddy Roosevelt. This episode was entirely unexpected and it happened on the Kaibab Forest in Arizona many years ago, in 1913. Alec Indian, who was a Piute Indian and one of the greatest cowboys I ever rode with or ever became acquainted with, was my partner this particular day. We were camped at VT Park on the Kaibab and we were assigned to ride the forest, bring in all the cattle that we could find, drive them into Park Lake, into the corrals which we had built there, brand the unbranded, and take out the steers which would be joined with the day herd for the trail to the railroad 350 miles away at Lund, Utah.

About midmorning we jumped about twenty head of cattle in the vicinity of Bright Angel, on the north rim of the Grand Canyon. They were wild and as they broke to run, they crashed the timber and made considerable noise. Our horses were trained for this event and knew exactly what to do. Alec was riding my right, I took the left, and our purpose was to follow that herd of cattle until they were winded and then come out in lead of them and, finally, as they gentled down, to turn them in the direction of the corral which was some six or seven miles away. As my horse broke into a fast run, he leaped over a very large, fallen pine tree. And, as we went over, I saw along the side of the pine tree a cougar feeding on a deer which he had just killed. My horse sensed the situation, and, as a horse is very much frightened of cougar, he decided that he did not want to light at all in that vicinity. He quivered in the air and almost shook me out of the saddle and when he did land he was really drifting.

I was letting out war whoops and my partner, Alec Indian, who was on the other side of the herd, but behind them, was shouting, too, with all the excitement that the occasion demanded. Letting out shrill war whoops as only Indians and real cowboys can do, we approached a group of horsemen and packs. We shouted louder as the cattle went by and we passed those men and horses, not knowing who they were and caring less because the cattle was our game and we had to round them up and bring them back into captivity.

We finally headed out these cattle and turned them, after a mile or two, down this canyon and got them winded and gentle enough so that they could be directed. And we drifted them up the canyon and onto a trail that led into the corrals at Little Park where we corralled them for the night. We then continued on to our camp at VT Park, laughing and kidding each other all the time about frightening to death our visitors to the Kaibab. But upon arriving at our camp, the cook told us that the party camped within several hundred yards of our camp was President Theodore Roosevelt and his party. Then we, of course, became serious and thought what an event we had been through that day to scare the President of the United States half out of his wits with our shouts and with the breaking of timber by the wild cattle as we dashed by him and his party.

The next morning I thought it would be in order to go to President Roosevelt's camp and apologize for the fright we had given him and his party the previous day. I approached him and told him who I was and that I wanted to apologize for the interruption which I'd made in his progress through the Kaibab Forest, and that in order to compensate, the cowboys, I said, would be happy if he would permit us to put on a rodeo for his entertainment. He said that would be one of the finest experiences of his visit and something he had not expected. But he said, "Today is Sunday," and he said, "I prefer to honor the Sabbath Day. And, if you will forgive me, I appreciate this offer, but I'd rather you didn't today."

I said, "President Roosevelt, tomorrow is another day. We didn't know it was Sunday today. Sorry." Cowboys never knew, or we did not in those days, know one day from another. We worked every day, seven days a week, thirty days a month, and that's all we knew. We had no communication, no letters, no nothing to inform us what day it was. That was before the days of sleeping bags, where we had only our blankets and tarpaulins. We did not have the luxury of even a tent. We laid out in the open under the trees if there were trees and out in the desert if we were in the desert. We trailed cattle, we branded cattle, we rounded them up and we branded the calves, and separated the ones that should go into the day herd to be trailed to the railroad in the fall of the year when the sales took place. And that was all we knew.

So, on the following day, we got some of the wildest cattle we had out of what we had corralled the previous day, and instead of separating them, turning them loose, we held them for this event. Fortunately, we had a wild, unbroken horse that had never been ridden and we decided, after roping the steers and riding some of them, we would ride this wild, unbroken horse. And I was the man that rode it. Two of the other cowboys helped me put the saddle on and then I mounted this horse and he really put on a good show for a few minutes. And then suddenly he reared over backwards, hoping to crush me as he came over. But I politely stepped off to one side and let him fall. At this point, I took off my cowboy hat and bowed toward the President and his party and at that time they gave me a great ovation, yelling and shouting and laughing like they really enjoyed it.

This was the end of an episode that began with a great scare for a President's party when they heard us rushing through and breaking down the timber as we came toward them in the little canyon toward Bright Angel. And it was the only time in my eighty years of experience on the earth that I have become personally acquainted with a President of the United States and had the honor of entertaining him, and also of having felt the great handclasp that he gave me.[36]

The Death of Yellow Hammie

I must tell you the story of my saddle horse, Hammie, Yellow Hammie. He was a yellow gelding, weighed about 1,000 pounds, and was trained to be a very fine cattle horse. He was a big, strong one. And I rode him one day when the cowboys in our outfit were gathering the east points of the Kaibab. They are the points that face and overlook the House Rock Valley country from North Canyon to Point Imperial of the Grand Canyon. And it's necessary every fall, after the first heavy snow, to gather these points to take the cattle off, as otherwise they stay and starve to death during the winter months. In fact, one point is called Carcass Point, and you cannot walk without stepping on bones of dead cattle. That's true. And horses, a lot of the wild mustangs drifted that way too, trying to get into the lower regions, you know, for the winter, and these points

[36]Rider adds, "I became acquainted with Kermit, President Roosevelt's son. In fact, he lived at my home in Kanab. I recommended that he stay there if he would like to remain a week or two. My sister Jen, who lived at home at that time, was very happy to have him as a guest."

have no escape route. You just go out on these points, like the ends of your fingers from the main mountain, and there's ledges all around them and it's only a matter of a week or two or three weeks probably at the most 'till the stock are all dead if they stay there because they eat what little foliage they can get to, then they starve to death. So, this became evident from observation and therefore the Bar Z outfit sent the cowboys up there every fall after the first big, heavy snowstorm, several days later, giving the cattle a chance to drift toward the House Rock Valley.

So we rode these points, and we rode North Canyon Point, and Carcass Point, which is rightly named as I've said, and then the next one south is Wildcat Point, and the next one south is South Canyon Point and then there's a long rim without any points projecting out over the valley below until you get to Saddle Mountain Point. The first day we covered everything from North Canyon to Wildcat Point, and Wildcat Point had a deer trail down it, from off of it, down through the sides of the ledge so you can get the cattle off there. That's the way we'd take the cattle down, down that trail down to the valley below. It was a very steep trail and difficult for the saddle horses to get up and men usually had to hang to the horses' tails in order to get up through it, it was that steep. But the second day the three boys that went out on Carcass Point got in a heavy snowstorm and were unable to get the cattle off of that point on account of the wind and the blowing snow. And that Carcass Point drops off for about a hundred yards at quite a steep angle, then projects out over the valley with sharp ledges all around. They found forty-five head of cattle out there and they tried to work them back up this slope that I just mentioned to get them up on top where they could drift south to Wildcat where they could drift them off, but they couldn't; the cattle wouldn't face the blizzard. And then they thought they'd get out themselves but their horses wouldn't face the blizzard either. Of course they'd exhausted the horses trying to get the cattle off. And the cowboys couldn't face it either, so they decided they'd have to lay there all night in these pine trees out on there; they were spruce, no dry wood, all green.

Well, they gathered up some tinder from under the trees and, after quite a few attempts, the cowboy whose name was Amos Wilson, who was nicknamed "Swift" because he was the slowest man I've ever known, with his very last match that he had, started the fire that saved the lives of those three cowboys. And I can still hear Nate Petty—he stuttered you know—I can still hear him telling us afterwards, "B-b-b-b-by G-G-God, it lit!"

So they kept piling on this fuel that they could break off from the trees all night long and kept themselves warm enough so they survived. But all three horses perished and the cowboys laid right in the legs of the horses, up against their bellies to keep warm, and they had a fire in there, but parts of the cowboys froze anyway, their wrists and their ears and necks were frozen.

Well, the other five cowboys down at the bottom of the ledges had a nice warm camp, plenty of firewood and plenty of forage for the horses who were hobbled out in the area. But we were concerned all night, so we didn't sleep, just built a big fire, hoping that these three cowboys would come. Their names were Johnny Wilson, his brother, Amos Wilson, the one we called "Swift," and Nate Petty from the little town of Rockville in southern Utah. The other two boys were from Kansas; they were cowboys from Kansas. As soon as daylight permitted, we wrangled three horses and we headed up the Wildcat Trail. The wind had stopped blowing, but it had blown all night, though, and it blew snow off the Kaibab in great drifts. Oh, the drifts would hang from the top ledges and go clear to the bottom of the valley, there was that much snow that had wiped clean off of the Kaibab, 'cause it had been snowing all day and there had

been about three foot of snow there. Anyway, by the time we got up on top, that was the normal. Well, we got up just to the top of the Wildcat Trail, and here came our three cowboys dragging their saddles behind them, heading for the trail down, to come down and tell us they were all right. It was over a mile down to our camp, right down that steep trail, yep. But anyway, we never thought we'd see them anymore, not alive. And of course the horses couldn't take it. They had been ridden and exhausted trying to get the cattle up that slope I told you about, to get 'em up on top so they could run along the rim with them and take them on the trail they come in on over the Wildcat Trail.

So we laid in camp all one day and thawed those three boys out, and it was storming all day and the wind ablowing up on top and we could see it blow clear out into the valley, that snow'd come out over. Anyway, you look out there and it would sprinkle your face with snow, and yet there was no snow down where we were; it was clear. But the wind was ablowing, oh boy, did it blow. Well, the next day eight of us went up the South Canyon Trail; that was a good trail because we drifted horses down there in the fall and every spring–out of the House Rock Valley and to Cape Royal where we had the summer range for the horses in the summertime. And that trail was not too steep because that South Canyon runs back toward the Kaibab, probably a mile and a half from the edge of the ledges, so it became a rather moderate-grade trail, easy to navigate when there wasn't any snow. So we headed up there and the boss divided the group up–all but three of us who went south toward Saddle Mountain Point to gather cattle, if there were any, and bring them back to South Canyon Trail and down the trail.

And it seemed to be a fine, quiet morning. The wind had died down and we had no trouble at all agetting up there except getting through some of the drifts on the side, a few of them. And as we turned south, we ran into bare ground where snow had been swept off of the entire top of the Kaibab, except where some trees and branches had held it back, and so we were on bare ground going down toward Saddle Mountain, south along this level rim–top of the ledge, you know. But, boy, about that time the wind started and here come the blizzard again, blowing snow for miles back across the Kaibab, bringing it through the trees just like it was falling from above, you know, and it was clear sky. I didn't think it was going to be too bad, but the other two boys said, "Oh, boy, the heck with the cattle; we're going back." But I said, "Well, I'm not going to quit. I'm going on; I might find a herd of cattle out there." In fact, they were two of the boys who had laid out all night and their horses froze, and they says, "We're not going through that again." So they went back.

Then I went on, facing the storm; it wasn't too bad right then. Boy, I hadn't got very far when my horse threw up his head and stopped. And while he was stopped there with his ears pointed, I heard a "moo," from a cow, you know. I listened again and sure enough, here was another "moo." So, I knew the direction to go, so I went a little further. I left Hammie, threw the reins over his head and I went down to where, I couldn't see any tracks, of course, but I went down in about a foot of snow down this slope. And I could see this overhanging ledge and I went down and went in the cave down there and there was seven head of cattle in there, and they were all down, starving to death; they was just down, couldn't get up. So I slit their throats out of mercy. They'd never get out of there. They'd been laying in there since the first storm hit, and probably three weeks before that when the first storm drove them out there and they missed the Saddle Canyon Trail.

So then I went back up to my horse and thought, "There must be some more cattle down here," so I went on down, along the rim and I got down to Saddle Point, and there was no cattle out there on it. And I assumed that these seven head were the only ones that had drifted out there and drifted down this little slope and got in this cave. And the storm got bad so I decided to turn around. My horse wouldn't go any further. He knew that the other horses had gone back. He didn't want to go. He couldn't face the storm anyway and neither could I. So we turned around. I thought we could get back to that cave and make it all right. It was filled with pine burs and small pieces of pine limbs and so forth that the squirrels and chipmunks had carried in there over the years and I knew it would be a good, dry place for us to stay. I could have made a fire, but it'd be warm anyway, and I could have laid in there with those dead cows. And of course there'd be room for Hammie too.

But when I got to where I thought the cave was, I couldn't see very well. I saw a little hump down there and I thought, "Well, that's the ledge above the cave," and I threw the reins down. So I started down that slope, pretty steep, and there was about a foot of snow, maybe two feet of snow on the slope there; the rest of it had been drifted on over on the main ledge which was a little further down. And I got right to where I thought I was right on top of the cave, and I heard old Hammie neigh. I looked up and there he was, shaking the reins ahead of him and coming down that slope, and I hollered "Hammie, Hammie, stop!" And just as I hollered at him, he lost his footing and he come down like a toboggan on that snow right down toward me and I jumped out of the way quickly, three or four feet, just about the time he would have hit me, jumped back right out of the line of traffic that he was in so he wouldn't hit me. And he went out of sight, and I went out of sight, about three feet from him. We were in a snowdrift. Instead of a ledge it was a snowdrift that had blowed over the edge of the cliff. And so I didn't know anymore for quite a long while. I went down through this snow and finally stopped. I knew I was falling straight down 'cause there's nothing but straight ledges. It was just like nothing, just soft, just like getting in a feather bed, just goin' down, just gently down quite fast then finally slowing up.

And the snow had piled up under my big cowboy hat with the strap under the chin, and it was choking me, and I got ahold of the strap with my fingers and dug this snow out and got my hat off so I could get the snow out of it. And I had just put my hat back on and I could see daylight out there, I could see the whole House Rock Valley right there, and just as I was looking out, bang, I went again. I started to go and I come out of the snowdrift clear down to the bottom of the mountain. And I came out about a rod from where Hammie came out, out of a little hole, not much bigger than three feet in diameter in the snow. And the hole he came out of was about a rod across, great big, it was about ten, fifteen feet in diameter where he came out of the snow bank. And after that he hit the slope, the slope that went off gradually into the valley, and he hit this and he skidded down that until he hit an oak that was high enough to stick out of the snow and it stopped him. So I just went on down to where he was and he was a bag of bones; there wasn't one unbroken bone in his body. The saddle was just tied to a bag of bones. Hammie had hit a projecting ledge, or maybe ledges, and I didn't; over where I went it was perpendicular, rocks projected out in the snowdrift that he was going in and he hit that ledge and mashed himself all to pieces. Those three feet when I jumped out of his way saved my life. If he hadn't neighed, I would've gone where he went. One more step and I would've been gone. I wouldn't be here telling you about it either!

Well, I took my saddle off and took my de-awelta (you use it to tie cattle up, you tie it around your waist, it's about three feet long) and hooked that to the horn of the saddle and drug it down, went on clear down and went over into camp. We had a good camp in the cedars, and when I come up the cook had a good fire down in there and I could see the smoke comin' up through the pine trees down there. And all those boys were looking up there thinking they'd never see me again. And when I walked in there, they all spilled their coffee. They sure let up a holler.

This took place in 1908 and I went back in there in 1921 to build a monument for Hammie, a rock monument, to put his skull in this monument, but I couldn't build it. I took two fellows with me, a cowboy and a friend, and we went to a water spring that I'd always known from where I'd camped before, expecting to find water, and it was dry. So we camped there anyway. It was nighttime, and the next morning we had to follow our horses about six miles back to find them. They'd gone for water, you know, back on the trail that we'd come over. They, of course, couldn't find any. Then we brought them back to camp and packed up and went up the Saddle Mountain Trail up on top of the Kaibab and over to Greenland Spring, this spring at Greenland. Greenland is where you go down to Cape Royal–last time we were there we saw ten head of bucks there, boy, they were big fellas. So that was the end of Yellow Hammie.

Roping Wild Steer

The whole bunch of us were riding on the Kaibab, gathering cattle for the sale in the fall at Pipe Springs. All the Kanab men that had cattle were riding with us, plus the Bar Z men. All together we gathered this whole mountain. And we struck some wild ones out here a little ways. They went down off of these ridges. And I caught a big, tremendous steer, the biggest steer that was ever seen on the mountain here. Golly, he was a whale. I forget how old he was now, quite old, but he was a big fellow, a big old red steer, bigger than my horse.

And I thought, "Oh, boy, I'm going to put a rope on him as soon as he gets to that open spot." And I did. I caught him and right around the horns, too, just a perfect catch. But I couldn't throw him because it was in the trees. And so I just let my horse stop him and let a tree come between him and the horse so the steer couldn't get to the horse. That steer fought just as soon as he turned around, why, he made a dive for my horse and my horse went on the other side of a quaking asp tree. It was a good thing he did. My horse was just standing on his hind legs, turning to get out of the way, you know. He was a great dapple gray horse named Boyce. And when the rope come tight, it threw Boyce down on his side and I just left my feet right there in the stirrups–I just sat right there on him. And then I held Boyce from getting up with the bridle reins so he couldn't get his head up and talked to him softly so he'd stay quiet a little.

I held him there for about four hours until that old steer'd let up on that rope. See, when that steer'd fight, then he'd back up a little, and I'd pull up a little of the rope around the tree and wrap it around the horn of the saddle. When I thought I had got enough slack on the steer so that I thought I had room to get up without my horse getting gored, then I chirped to my horse and let his rein loose and my horse jumped up. But boy, that old steer made a high dive. And he was so close and he was mad and he frothed at the mouth and he'd just blow that froth all over me. But my horse was a good one and we got that steer under control and we took him into Mile-and-a-Half to await the others.

Well, in the meantime, six or eight of the other boys caught a steer with a Quarter Circle X brand, the brand of the Taylor Button or Robbers Roost gang, as it was called, and it had been fifteen or eighteen years since that brand had ever been run on cattle. That's how old that steer was. Well, the funny thing about that Quarter Circle X steer was that they neck roped him to a two-year-old steer so they could bring him into their herd and take him into Mile-and-a-Half there at the corrals. And the two steers were running along, tied together, and the little one run under the old one's neck, back and forth, and the old one stepped on the two-year-old and broke his own neck. So that's why they didn't come back to me. That's why they was so dang long. They cut this Quarter Circle X's throat and bled him and skinned him and hung up all the meat in the trees around there. Next day, we sent the packs over there to get him and we made jerky out of that meat.[37] By golly, there was a ton of it there. Everybody had all their saddle pockets and their own pockets full of jerky on that trip.

Well, when they brought a bunch of that wild band in, then they turned the steer I'd caught loose; one of the boys pulled out his hind legs and we took my rope off. Well, then that steer took after my horse and followed him. He wouldn't look at any other horse. And by golly, he stayed behind my horse's tail and we led that herd, twenty head of cattle, I think there was, right into Mile-and-a-Half where we were camped, right into the corral. All that way. And my horse pranced all the way in there, looking back at that steer, afraid he was going to get gored.

From then on, from there to Jacob's Lake where we camped, we'd have to take the cattle out and day herd them so they could eat. And then at night we'd drift them into the corral. But when they'd herd this old one, he'd never eat, that big steer wouldn't. He never ducked his head down to take a bite of food. And you could look out at that big herd, 3,000 head of steers, and you could see that feller standing shoulders above all the others, about a foot above any other critter in the herd. He was proud. He'd never been roped and he was an old steer and he wouldn't eat a bite.

And when they started to drift from one place to another, from Mile-and-a-Half to Three Lakes, or from there to Jacob's Lake, he was always right on lead, pointing the herd. Boy! And he went from Jacob's Lake down to Jacob's Canyon on the way to Pipe Springs[38]—and he died walking. The boys that were on the trail with him said that steer just died standing up, a-walking, just keeled over in his tracks and died. Never ate a bite, broke his heart when I roped him.

---

[37] I asked Rider how they made jerky and he replied, "Just boil salt water, make brine out of it, and then just dip the meat in and hang it up on the limbs around."

[38] Pipe Springs is where they would sell the cattle. Rider says this steer was worth twenty-three dollars. "That's all they'd give for a big steer in those days. Cows and calves sold for seventeen dollars."

Riding The Points

There was approximately 60,000 head of cattle on the Kaibab Forest in 1908 and '09, 150 to 200 saddle horses and ten cowhands, cowboys, experts all of them, to herd and move and wean the calves and, generally speaking, to drift the cattle from the winter to the summer ranges on the Kaibab and to brand the calves and to gather the steers in the fall of the year and to drift them off the Kaibab to the nearest railroad, which is Lund, Utah, a 175-mile drift from Jacob's Lake.

But every year (since the Kaibab Forest, or the southern part of it, is a plateau with sharp points breaking into deep, steep canyons, really box canyons, all the way around) it was necessary each fall for ten cowboys, after the first snowstorm, to make sure all the cattle had drifted to the points or were off the winter ranges without any trouble, that no cattle were lost in those areas. It was necessary then, that these ten men, five on each side, five on the east side, five on the west side, would come from the winter headquarters after the first heavy snowstorm, which is usually the latter part of November, to make sure the cattle were drifted. This drive to gather them off the points wouldn't be successful unless it was late enough to make sure all of them had drifted to the points. So the ten men, with five horses each and a pack mule or pack horse each, would get their equipment ready at Kane.

All the horses had to be shoed and the packs had to be shoed also and the provisions had to be loaded in each man's pack according to what his pack could carry. And these provisions had to last at least three weeks, with what deer could be killed on the way to supplement the food that we carried in the packs, because there was no other source of supply on this three-week trip. So the boys would leave after everything was ready, they would leave Kane at daylight, first part of December, usually, and climb the mountain straight west up the gradual slope of the Kaibab to Pleasant Valley. The first night, they would cut quaking asp trees to feed the horses on the point just east of Pleasant Valley. The next day, they'd fight through the snow to VT Park where we had a big cabin. That was the summer headquarters. And then they'd make camp there and go on the ridge just east of the cabin up on the side hill and cut quaking asps for the horses there. It would take a full day to go from Kane to

Pleasant Valley Point and a full day through the snow to VT Park headquarters and a full day from there to Robbers Roost Canyon without food for the horses except for the quaking asps that they would eat. And sometimes the horses wouldn't eat for two or three days.

And it was difficult work because the snow was deep up through the mountain, that snow was up to the horse's forelocks, five to ten feet deep, and each man rode his horse until he was tired, or getting tired. And then he would take the next horse back of him and he would ride him until he was tired, ride him without a bridle or a saddle, and then he'd take the next one back of him and so forth until he rode his five. And the cowboy back of him would be coming up then in line and he would ride his saddle horse, with his saddle, until he gave out and then he'd take the next horse back, kick him out of the trail and let him fight, so on and so forth, until all five men rode the twenty-five horses. And the packs followed behind in the trail we made through this deep snow.

And when we got down to Robbers Roost Canyon, there was a deer trail under the first rim and there was a lot of grass down there. So at the end of the third day, the horses had some grass to eat and we'd lay there one day and let the horses tank up on this grass on this deer trail under the ledges in a little valley. And it was not much of an area, but it produced a lot of grass. And then we'd pack up and move and draw cuts, usually, to see who went left toward the east rim, toward Bright Angel and Cape Royal and Saddle Mountain and South Canyon Points, Wildcat Point, Grass Point, Gooseneck Point and North Canyon Point, and those that went west to Sublime Point, which is the next point west of Robbers Roost Canyon where we divided. So five men went each way and we divided the packs and the horses.

This particular winter, I went west and we drifted all day down to Point Sublime after we left Robbers Roost Canyon where the horses had a chance to eat and get rested up for a whole day. In the meantime, the cowboys rolled rocks off the ledges for entertainment. Then we made camp down on Sublime Point, well, not quite down on the point, but back up in the quaking asp trees, about a mile and a half away from the end of the point. We got down there before the sun went down and two of us made camp and the other three went down on the point to see if there was any cattle and to bring them back up this mile and a half or two miles up to where our camp was. And they found forty-eight head of cattle on this point and drifted them back up to where our camp was and pushed them a little beyond our camp toward the next point, west and north, and then we laid there; we had a good dinner that night. But the wind had been blowing for about two and a half days all up through the VT Park and the Pleasant Valley, and it blowed all this night.

And it started to snow just before daylight and we knew we were in for bad trouble because we had all the snow we could handle then. And so we packed up and without giving the cattle another thought, we drifted out toward Swamp Point and Powell Plateau, or the Powell Saddle; that was a point where we knew we could get to lower elevation and our only salvation was to get out of the country. It had never been done before and, therefore, we traveled all day without getting breakfast. And that night at sundown, we hit the Swamp Canyon, which was quite a deep canyon, and we drifted down that for about a mile and a half or two miles, the distance is indefinite in my mind, through the deep snow.

And it was snowing all day just as hard as it could snow. Each man rode his five horses and then the next man in turn took it so that they all had equal distribution of work, all the horses did, except the packs and, of course, they just trailed along in the trail we plowed for them. And we were all wet. Boy, we were just wringing wet all the time, riding on wet horses, and snow, you know, would pile on us. The snow would come off the trees, blow off of them and fall. It snowed all the way across there, snowed all day just terrifically, just piled up the snow all day and we were just as sopping wet as you would be if you jumped in a swimming pool.

We laid down at the end of Swamp Canyon. This canyon, if we had continued, would have gone right into the Grand Canyon itself and, of course, it was necessary for us to stop before we got there. And the snow stopped about dark that night and so we left our saddles on our horses, took the packs off the pack saddles and loosened the belts on the saddle horses and left them all standing in a row in this trench in about six feet of snow. And we laid down our tarpaulins in the snow, dug out a place underneath the big pine trees where the snow wasn't very deep, because all the snow had piled up on the branches, and that's the way we made our beds down that night.

And Joe Miller, a cowboy from Kansas, got his tarpaulin out; he dug the snow away by the tree and got his tarpaulin spread out under the blankets and laid his blankets down and just as he had them spread out, a limb at the top of that tree let go and all the snow that had piled up in that tremendous tree came down, piled up fifteen feet of snow over his bed. And he was fighting for breath and we were fighting from the outside trying to dig in to him and he come out crying and I don't mean crying, I mean he was really "boo-hooing" and he said that if he ever got out of this trip alive, he was going back to Kansas and look an old mule in the hind end down the corn rows the rest of his life. Anyway, we got him quieted down, got his blankets out and shook the snow out of them and got his bed down and we all went to bed there without supper. We couldn't make a fire, too much snow and we were too nervous, anyway. So our horses stood still right there in their tracks all night long.

And next morning the boss hollered, "All out," and we all threw back our tarpaulins. There was only just two or three inches of snow that had come in the night. It had quit about the time we got there, almost anyway. But when I rared up (there was Ed Chalk there on one side and Joe Miller on the other), when I rared up, well, lo and behold, there were those forty-eight head of cattle right in the trail standing right there just like our packs–in order. By golly, here they followed us out.

Well, we began our daily task of loading up without trying to prepare breakfast or anything. We just took some cheese and some raisins and stuff and that's all each man had in his chap pockets to eat because we didn't want to waste any time getting out of the country. And we looked around and Ed Chalk hadn't moved under the snow. His tarpaulin was still out there and I went over there and said, "Come on, Ed," and I kicked his tarpaulin. It was like a board. And I said, "You've got to get out of there; the rest of us are almost packed." He said, "I can't move a limb." I got down and pulled his tarpaulin off of him and I said, "What's the matter?" and he said, "I don't know." I knew he'd been wet all day the day before coming through that snow and he'd been wet all up for three days prior to that coming up to Robbers Roost Canyon and I supposed he was just stiff or something, but he said, "No, I can't, I can't move." He said, "You'll have to take care of my pack."

And so we did. We got him out of his bed, he slept with his clothes and his boots on like we all did and they were partly dry; they'd dried out through the night a little bit. But he couldn't move. We had to lift him around. And he just begged me to let him stay there and die. "I can't move a muscle," he said, "let me die." He'd holler and yell but my brother, Dave, and I, we put him on a horse called Ball, one of the strongest horses out of the twenty-five saddle horses we had. And he was a skittish horse, but, oh, he was a fine roper and he belonged to my brother and no one had ever ridden him until that day and we put this man, Ed Chalk, on him. Ed was about thirty-five years old then and I was eighteen and we put him on this horse and that was my job to put him up on that horse and to tie him on: put his saddle on Old Ball and see that it was properly cinched up and to put him on and tie his hands to the horn and to tie his feet underneath. And he just hollered. He gritted his teeth when I would tie his hands to the saddle horn.

In the meantime, doing this, the rest of the leaders, the rest of the horses and the packs, had gone on. They had taken a long, gradual slope from this point in the bottom of the canyon, where we laid down for the night, and they went gradually up toward the rim of the canyon, up onto Swamp Point, and followed a trail that we picked

so the horses could make it up the incline without going directly to the right and climbing straight up. They could never have pulled it, they couldn't get up, they weren't strong enough, so we took a long, sloping climb out so they'd be able to navigate. And my brother led them. He knew the way and he led them up through this long slope and went on.

And I was there with this sick man that couldn't move, tying him on, and the forty-eight head of cattle that we had rounded up down on Sublime was in the trail, single file, forty-eight of them strung out behind us. They were waiting to go, too. When we moved, they all come, too. So when they saw the packs going, they wouldn't wait for me to get this cowboy, Chalk, on Old Ball. They broke a new trail around us there for a rod in the snow and they went on by, all forty-eight head went by and up this incline trail in the snow that the rest of the horses and the packs had plowed. And by the time the last one got by, I had got on my horse and started off and Ed Chalk's horse followed me and I followed right behind these cattle.

As I got up there a little ways, maybe a five minute ride, I saw the cattle was going down the sidehill, sliding sideways, going end for end, just going down in all directions, sliding right off into the canyon. And I could see them kicking their legs and switching their heads as they went off and out of sight down into the canyon below. They went a long ways in mid-air before they disappeared from my view down over the ledge. See, they were going so fast they sailed right out in the air, you know, and they went over the brink and they went quite a ways kicking before they disappeared and went down into the canyon. And every one would go, every one. That hill was as slick as glass after the first ones went.

When I got closer, I saw the last cow was a cow with a calf and the calf was ahead of the cow and the calf made it, he went across this slick spot, which was only about six feet long, and the calf got across it all right. But his mother, the last cow in the string, slipped and hung on a minute, and then away she went and she bellered as she went sliding, like a cow would do, you know, calling for her calf, and the calf turned around and took after her down that slope. It was just like a toboggan slide. That calf run four or five good jumps down that hill and then he lost his footing and he just went end for end like a cartwheel over and over, kicking as he went out of sight, down out of my vision, down over the ledge.

They all slipped in the same cockeyed spot within six feet. And there was two Hereford bulls that cost over $1,000 apiece to get them into this country by trailing them in from Nebraska, by railroad part way and then by trailing them by slow stages. In those days there was no cattle trucks to haul them from the railroad. They had to be trailed by cowboy, you know, so far a day and then fed at night or turned into a pasture somewhere along the road. And they had been trailed and were very valuable animals and there was two of them. One of those got just about through, he plowed kind of a new trail for himself, but he slipped and just before he went over the ledge, there was a small pine tree. I judged it must have been about a foot in diameter down there. And he hit that and his head went on one side and his body went on the other, he was going that fast. Yes, they split and there the head was going and here he was kicking his body and his head going along with it at the same time and they were separated. That was all of him.

I stopped there and watched them go, and old Ed sat up there gritting his teeth. I said, "Ed, what do you want to do?" And he says, "Just release my hands." And I said, "Okay." "And my feet, too," he says. I put my lariat on him and I says, "I'll wait. I'll see if old Ball makes it." And I kicked the snow out of Ed Chalk's horse's hooves; I led him up to the side of me and my horse and picked up his feet and where the snow had all gone in there I dug it down with my boots. Then I got a rock that was loose there and I took that rock and I hammered the hooves of the horses and got the snow that had caked in them so the hooves wouldn't slip on the caked snow, you know, so the shoe would have a chance to hang. And then I untied Ed's feet and his hands from the saddle and then I put my lariat around his body and I stayed there so that if his horse slipped, I could pull Ed off and he wouldn't go down the slide. But, fortunately, Old Ball went just as carefully as he could across. It seems like he sensed what was up. He'd watched all those cattle, that horse had, he'd watched them all slide and he just was as careful as he could be and he just took one foot right after the other and he made it. And then I led my horse across. I walked in front of him because I didn't want him to trip and throw me if I had hold of his tail. So I just walked carefully. I just made him go right slow and I went right slow and carefully, and boy, that old horse just followed me all the way across. And he didn't slip because I'd kicked the snowballs that caked up under their shoes, you know, like they do in the snow. And so we got across.

And then I tied Ed's hands and feet again to Ball, got on my horse, and took the lead. We had a good trail then clear on down to the point, down to South Pass Saddle. And I hadn't seen any of the men since before I loaded Ed on his horse. They'd left, you see, and then the cattle all went by and I watched them go down the slide. When I got about a mile from the top, after I come out of this dangerous place and went along on the level Swamp Point down through the pine on the trail that had been made, our horses could go rather fast because they didn't have to buck snow, they had a pretty good trail. And they would step in the other horses' tracks, too, they'd learned how to step in their tracks as they went and that helped too.

We got down there about a mile from the top where we stopped out there and here was a yearling more than a little over a year old, about a twelve- or fourteen-month-old heifer, very fine flesh because she had had plenty to eat all summer and only had two hard days coming across through that snow. I didn't know it had got by that slide, didn't see any of them get by. But she did. But she couldn't keep up, couldn't go as fast as I wanted to, and so I nudged her a little and the horse bit her tail and she turned around to fight and when she did that horse just pushed her out of the way into the snow and went on. We went on and left her there and thought that it was the last we'd see of her.

But anyway we went on down and caught the rest of the packs and the horses just at the top of the Powell Saddle, at the end of Swamp Point. And my horse was fresh, hadn't been working all day, only carrying me along you know. He didn't have to fight the snow like the others had and so I got in front with him and I plowed a trail down. We just went right straight off down into Powell's Saddle without winding back and forth, just went off. There was enough snow to hold him from slipping over the rocks or the ledges or the brush or anything. And he just slid down there, half on his haunches, you know, went on down there, plowing snow about eight, nine feet deep, right off into that saddle. And at the bottom of the saddle I turned right and I broke trail, then, because he was fresh, my horse and I broke trail about a mile and a half to the first bunch of quaking asp trees that we found down in Stynie's (this is a place down under the ledges there).

And when I got to these trees, I knew that was the feed for our horses. If we ever expected to ride them out of there, we had to get some quaking asp trees. That was the only thing that they would eat. They wouldn't eat anything else. All the oak leaves were gone. They would eat those, boy, they loved those, but there wasn't any here. The frost and the snow had caused them to fall off.

So we camped there for twenty-one days and we cut trees every day for those horses and they ate every little limb up to about a quarter of an inch in diameter and they'd peel all the bark off of the big limbs and the main trunk of the tree with their teeth. They'd just trim them, all they could get on the upper sides, you know. And then each day we'd go out and cut some more for them and that kept them alive but they were skin and bone, they couldn't carry a man, they were too weak; you could just pull them down by taking hold of the top of their forelock, and just by giving them a quick jerk sideways, they'd go right down in the snow and then you'd have to help them up.

After we got down there, there was five feet of snow at the bottom, down under Stynie, and we had our camp shovels and we took these little short-handled shovels and we shoveled that snow out of a circle about ten feet in diameter. And after we'd got it all shoveled out, we had about twelve feet of snow and then we dug five igloos, one for each man to put his tarpaulin and his blankets in, and we slept in these igloos for twenty-one days and took care of this sick man. Had to feed him, like a baby, you know; he could move his jaws, that was all. He couldn't twist his head; couldn't move his arms. And we made Brigham tea, we got some Brigham tea down there and we fed him Brigham tea. He liked coffee, but I got him drinking this Brigham tea. That's what I drink. Boy, it was good.[39]

---

[39]Later, when I asked what Brigham tea was, Rider explained, "The Indians drank it, and so they told Brigham Young about how good it was and so now we call it after Brigham Young, we call it Brigham tea. I can't think of the name that the Indians called it. You just boil water with these little, short stems. They're like jointed stems, little joints on them, like a fishing pole, you know. It's a little bush. . . . Boy it was lovely with sugar. I wouldn't like it without, but I sure did drink it. And it's a good tonic in the springtime. I've drank it for years. I have a whole bag of it now in my basement, down in my storeroom."

But, anyway, the next morning I was the first one awake and I looked out from my igloo, wasn't five feet from my head where the fire was, and standing over the still-hot coals of our fire of the night before where we had cooked a good meal, first one in three days, was this heifer, standing right square over the coals. And so we killed her and that kept us from killing our pack horses to eat because we would have run out of food without that critter down there. So by an act of God, one out of forty-eight head of cattle followed us down, her own self, followed us, and stood over the fire ready to be butchered and provide us with food over this long twenty-one day stretch.

We had to ration our food, by the way. We only had so much flour, and so much cheese (we had some of these round cheese, about that big around, with a kind of a cloth on them, cheesecloth on them), and so much dried fruit, and rice, and raisins. And that was our menu, because we'd expected to kill deer, which we always had done previous years, for meat. But this critter, this yearling, made very good meat and we even roasted the head and ate the jaws, ate every bit of food that there was on that beast.

And we had a campfire going day and night. We had good, dry wood for our fires, cut it down off the trees. It was laying around there. There were dead trees lying just like there is always, and they were dry. Boy, we didn't have any trouble. We'd find kindling and dry needles every morning, you know, and we threw them on the coals. We covered the fire up at night with our little hand shovel and the next morning we'd just dig it out and throw that kindling in and we'd have a fire in two seconds. And we melted snow over this fire for our water.

So we had fire, water and some food, but we never thought that we would get out of there. No one did. I didn't think that we would ever make it out. I didn't have anything to write on or I didn't have a pencil to write with so I couldn't write anything. We had hopes if our horses didn't live, or were too poor to pack us out, that we could go around those ledges and come out at the Big Saddle and maybe by packing enough of our food with us on our backs, that we could make this little ranger station down there that we call Jump Up. Probably, but we weren't sure if we could, but we had been thinking about that out loud. We'd say, "Maybe we could make it afoot." Boy that's a long way, wow!

One cowboy lost his button. He got to cursing the Lord and I had to rebuke him for profanity, and I had to do it in the name of Jesus Christ. I just told him. I commanded him, in other words. And it just quieted him down and he shook like a leaf and he never swore anymore on that trip. That was the end of it. But it's a wonder that we all didn't go nuts down there.[40]

When that yearling was gone, we began to draw cuts to see which pack horse we'd eat and you know we got old Deadman. He killed a man–and when he threw him off and fell, it broke his hind leg. And for the life of me I don't now how that leg ever mended but it did. And he was a good pack horse. He'd stand still and he'd carry a big load although he limped quite a bit with that hind leg. But he plowed through the snow with the pack on him just fine. And we were going to kill him. We had five pack animals and we had a stick for each one from Deadman on down, the longest one was old Deadman. And when we drew these, I forget who drew Deadman's, but he was the one that we were going to kill.

See, there's no deer down in there. But we could see deer way up. We could see them when they jumped in the air. We couldn't see them after they landed in their trail, but when they made a jump coming around there, you could see them above the snow, kicking as they'd land. Lying right down in the bottom there, you could see the stars in the daytime, looking straight up. And I was looking up and I saw these deer coming around in the snow, going around that sidehill. They knew there was ledges there, too, you know. And they come around, I guess, 'till they could come down. I don't know how far they come around or they might have come clear around and found our trail, I don't know. Clear up on this ledge trying to come,

---

[40]In another version, Rider mentions that he was the only one in the bunch that kept the Word of Wisdom, the health code of the Mormon Church which forbids smoking, drinking alcohol, tea and coffee, and advocates doing all things in moderation. I asked him if the others were Mormons. His reply was "Oh, no. Joe Miller wasn't and Ed Chalk was kind of a Jack Mormon. He drank more coffee than water. My brother [David Rider], of course, was a Mormon. He was baptized when eight. He'd been on the range all of his life. The only thing that he drank was tea. He didn't swear. He never cursed, and he was a good cowman. He was the boss of the Bar Z. He said when to go, where to go, and what to do. And Orin Judd was a baptized Mormon. He was the one that I had to rebuke. Joe Miller wasn't any faith. He's the one that said he'd watch that old mule go down that row of corn. And Ed Chalk was, like I said, a Jack Mormon, inactive in the Church. He was a cattleman, too. But he never drank or cursed hardly in his life since he was a kid."

coming right toward our trail. Rows of them. You could see them jump when they'd jump out of the snow. See, they'd drifted off, out of the forest, and couldn't go any further when they hit the ledge, so they went around the hill. And I could see them up there from down where we were, and I called it to the attention of the other four cowboys. Boy, we watched up there.

On the twenty-first day, we figured that we could make it without killing Deadman. We needed him to pack. He wouldn't have been very good to have eaten, anyway, because he was nothing but skin and bones. We knew we'd have enough provisions then, when we'd get out of there. We knew that if we could make that Big Saddle that we'd only be a short distance from all kinds of deer. So we crawled out on New Year's Day. Of course, we all had to walk, we couldn't ride our horses. There wasn't a one who could hold us up. Only man that rode was Ed Chalk; we loaded him on Old Ball again, he still seemed to be the strongest horse—put Chalk and his saddle up there and tied him on, and then we started at daylight.

The snow had been melting because the west part of that mountain was almost sheer and the afternoon sun from noon on shone right directly against it. And it melted the snow way down, so we only had about a foot of snow to travel that twenty-first day, most

places only about a foot deep. And then we went zigzagging back across what we call Stynie's over to what we call the Big Saddle country, and we knew there was an Indian trail out of there. And that was the place we were heading for in hopes that we could climb afoot if our horses couldn't, or our packs couldn't, get out.

But when we got over there, it faced south, and the snow there wasn't nearly as deep as it was down where we'd camped, nowhere near. And so we could pick out a pretty good trail and the horses didn't have to fight anything but wet soil and we picked out a zigzag trail and finally got up on top of the saddle. And we knelt down and prayed and built a big fire and I made candy for the cowboys out of sugar that we had rationed and baking powder. It wasn't very good candy but they ate it.

And the next day, we drifted the horses, they were still weak, and we'd ride a little ways and get off and walk and then we took them down to a deer trail that my brother knew down under what we called the Jump Up. Well, when we got down over there, of course, there were all kinds of deer, my golly, they were just dying of old age. We went down that deer trail and while we were camped down there, there would be a hundred head of deer, right there in sight of us, right there in camp. You never saw so many deer. Boy, I took after a big old buck. I run him out of camp. Then the old son-of-a-gun died. He died of old age. Just because he had to make a few jumps, his heart failed him and he died right there. Gee, he had tremendous horns, wow. He must of been old because he didn't have any teeth. I don't know how he got so fat. Gee, he was an old fellow. He could only make ten jumps and then he died. That was the first deer that I ever saw die from old age; he actually died running ten big jumps and then he was dead. He didn't make eleven.

And down there, the grass was up to the horses' knees and those horses just run back and forth and neighed to each other; they'd eat a bite or two and then they'd neigh again to each other. That grass had never been eaten. Deer had been down in there, but, boy, those horses just neighed, oh, boy, they neighed to each other and they'd grab a mouthful. We left them there five days, filling up and regaining some of their strength.

But on the third day we put this sick man on Old Ball again, and my brother took him to a ranger station, what we called Jump Up ranger station, and there they had a little cabin down there with a stove in it and they had a telephone, a one-wire telephone and they telephoned to the ranger station at Ryan. And they in turn telephoned to Fredonia, Arizona, and they got the sheriff, Thomas Jensen, with a white-topped buggy to come out and pick Ed up and they took him to Fredonia and doctored him at the hotel there for a number of weeks. He got a little better, so that he could travel on a wagon, and his folks from Tropic come down the Paria Creek and got him. That's what we heard later. It didn't do any good. He died anyway when they got him back. Inflammatory rheumatism, he couldn't move a joint, you know. All swelled up, his joints did. It nearly killed everybody.

That's the end of the twenty-one days and today–what's the date today, September 7, it's Labor Day–we're down on Swamp Point, just about five miles from where the saddle trail goes down, camping for the night, and our sleeping bags are all laid down and we've had a good cold lunch out of some kind of canned meat and raisin bread and one-third of a cantaloupe and a good drink of water. And, we have been down on this saddle today and Deirdre Murray and David Paulsen, who are with me, went down the trail, tried to get to these two bunches of quaking asp patches. There's only two of them in that whole country and if they hadn't of been there, we wouldn't have had any horses. So that was the ending of this long, twenty-one day period in one spot. And we're trying to seek today the pictures of the place where the forty-seven slipped off and went sprawling into the canyon, kicking as they went, in mid-air. So we're trying to get to this point where we can take a pictue of the toboggan slide, I call it, where they slipped and went over. Good night. See you tomorrow.

The Lone Timber Wolf

Uncle Jim Owens, who was the government trapper, trapped cougars, or mountain lions as they're called, on the Kaibab Forest in order to preserve the deer population.[41] He trained his dogs to trace

[41]But Rider later interjects how this government plan was successful to a fault. "And then the deer increased so that there were thousands of head of deer; you just couldn't go anywhere without seeing deer going in all directions. Well, then, they were feeding on the range here, too, and that was one reason why the cattlemen got off of here. So dang many

and to tree these lions and after they were treed, it was an easy matter to shoot them and to skin them. He got twenty-five dollars a head for them, bounty from the state of Arizona; twenty-five dollars each, whether they were adults or kittens, it didn't make any difference. All he was required to take for evidence to get his pay was the paws with the bone joints right in their paws. That's all he had to present. The last time I talked to Uncle Jim Owens, he told me he had captured 1,165 lions, and I'm not kidding, no, because he could catch one about every day.[42]

Now those dogs of Owens', they were good. But one day, they came up missing from Bright Angel. Owens was camped at the Little Bright Angel cabin at Bright Angel Springs about a mile and a half from the now famous Bright Angel resort center there on Bright Angel Point. His dogs took off, in the night, and for four days he didn't know where they were. He had tried to train them when he was tracking not to follow coyote tracks, nor bobcat tracks, but only to follow the scent of the cougar. But this was somewhat of a difficult job. I'll tell you this little story to represent this, of how these dogs got sidetracked and followed a wolf's tracks.

I was going from Jacob's Lake to VT Park on horseback and, in that area, there was the advent of a timber wolf, the only one that had ever been known to come into that country. Never had one been killed or trapped. But somehow this timber wolf migrated into that Kaibab area and he would kill about once a day, although he never went back to feed on his kill. He would kill cattle, calves and

---

deer, they just cleaned out this forest; you could see through it for miles. You know, no underbrush meant no browsing for the cattle. Those deer ate everything they could stand on their hind legs and reach."

[42]Angus M. Woodbury, "A History of Southern Utah and Its National Parks," *Utah Historical Quarterly* 12 (July-October 1944), p. 192, says that between 1906 and 1923 government hunters were provided to hunt the predatory animals on the Kaibab and that during that period "more than eight hundred cougars, thirty wolves, nearly five thousand coyotes and more than five hundred bobcats were removed." He continues: "One of the interesting characters among these hunters was 'Uncle' Jim Owen, who with his hounds took about six hundred cougars from the Kaibab and one hundred and thirty from regions to the north and west. He had previously been a member of the Jesse James gang and when intoxicated was a man to be avoided. At El Tovar, one night, he took a dislike to the clerk, tried to shoot him, and filled the room so full of holes it cost the party $100 to settle the damages."

heifers, and the ones that I've seen were aways young stock. His track had been seen from Jacob's Lake clear to VT Park, then it crossed over and down into Dry Park and down through Nail's Canyon and back up to Jacob's Lake through Warm Springs Canyon; so apparently he'd go in a circle. My brother saw him chasing a two-year-old steer one day near Crane Lake; my brother didn't have a gun but he dashed toward him and shouted and so forth and scared him away. So my brother knew then he was a timber wolf. But he was the only one that had seen him, as far as we knew.

I was camped at Crane Lake and we had about 3,000 head of mooing cattle in the corrals there, tremendous corrals. And it was in the fall of the year, it was in the drift time of the year, and we had been collecting steers to drift to Lund, Utah, to be sold, then to be shipped on the railroad to L.A. There was about fifteen cowboys there, eight or ten of them from Kanab and some of us from the Bar Z outfit. And when we were all sound asleep, the sound of this wolf, which none of us had previously heard, chilled everybody, and it chilled me, too. This timber wolf opened up on a little saddle just east of Crane Lake, about a quarter of a mile from where we were sleeping, and on the first howl we all reared up out of our tarpaulins. My good friend, the cook, who was named Johnny Kitchen, he took his bedroll on about the third or fourth howl and he drug it into an old salt shed there that was full of mud and muck where the cattle had waded in and out to lick the salt. He was that frightened. He just pulled his tarpaulin right over into this old muddy shack and there he stayed for the rest of the night.

And 3,000 head of mooing cattle stopped at the first or second howl. There wasn't a sound. And every cowbell on the mules, in the meadow there were mules who were grazing and their bells were tinkling as we went to our beds, stopped and were hushed. Nothing moved, not even a hoot owl. And that was a bloodcurdling event. I'll tell you, I'll never forget it as long as I live.

Now the next year, I was going from Jacob's Lake to VT Park again. There were no roads in those days, just a trail where the cattle drifted. And in the sand of that trail to VT Park were these great wolf prints, tremendous footprints, and I followed them from Crane Lake all through Pleasant Valley. They were right in the trail I was following with my pack and my horse. And as I got up to the south end of Pleasant Valley, I saw a tent pitched in a little bunch of quaking asp trees and I wondered why there was no smoke or no sign of a campfire because I saw the horses and pack horses grazing close by. They were hobbled. But I couldn't see any other sign of life. Now I had left Jacob's Lake early that morning, probably a little after daylight–it's a long ride from there to VT Park going horseback–and it must have been about noon when I got to this point I'm talking about where I saw this tent pitched in the trees, off about 100 yards from the trail. As I approached it, I looked down the trail and I saw where this wolf had sat down and his tracks were marred there a little bit and beyond that point I never saw his tracks again. So I knew that he must have stopped there and diverted his line of travel off of this trail toward this tent.

Well, when I got near, someone opened the flap of the tent and hollered at me, and I rode over to see what was wrong and they said, "We're frightened to death. We heard the most bloodcurdling thing that we have ever heard in our lives and we daresn't even go and get our packs off our horses. We've been here all morning afraid to go out." And they said, "We just couldn't sleep a wink from that time until daylight. And we thought at daylight we could look around, but we still daresn't come out and we're sure glad you come along."

And I said, "You know what it was?" And they said, "No, tell us." And I said, "I followed it from Crane Lake clear to here; I've been following for six or eight miles now the track of a great timber wolf. And he sat down right there and that's where he was howling at you." And they said, "Thank God you come."

All right, I'll tell you about Jim Owens's dogs now. I went on to VT Park and I told the cowboys there about these people afraid to leave their tent and they had a good laugh because some of them, also, had heard that cry that night at Crane Lake a year previous and they said, "I don't blame them at all." And I didn't myself. I knew just how those people must have felt that were strangers in the country and had never heard such a noise before; there's something powerful in a voice that'll even command the attention of his fellow animals. Well, I stayed with the rest of the cowboys there at VT Park and about three weeks later the story of Uncle Jim Owens, who had lost his dogs for four days, was brought to my attention by one of his nephews, Bob Vaughn, who helped him in this precarious work of hunting mountain lions. And he told us that on the fourth day all of the dogs came limping back to Bright Angel. All their feet were sore and they couldn't move, hardly, but they come home of their own accord. Apparently, they had got scent of this timber wolf when he come down to Bright Angel there; they'd taken his track and they'd barked and frightened him and chased him clear out of the country. They chased him for four days at least and they never would stop; once on a trail they would just go and go and go. And they chased that timber wolf out of the Kaibab into the sand hill country, which is just off the north end of the Kaibab and to the east toward Glen Canyon and toward Lee's Ferry. It's a different geographic area entirely than the Kaibab, all sand. And then the cattlemen over there began to find their cattle killed and they found the wolf's tracks, see.

So the cowmen in Kanab that run their cattle out there, Uncle Jet Johnson, Uncle Bill Hamblin, Walt Hamblin, and Zara Hamblin, and several other large cattle owners that run cattle in that country, offered a $1,000 reward for this wolf. So all the cattlemen got together and they stationed themselves across the barrier, which is only about seven miles long from Paria, where it cuts into the solid rock, to Two-Mile where the fault scarp starts. Nothing could pass it, not even a coyote, and they lined themselves across this area and they all had their rifles on their saddles. They knew from the fresh kills that this wolf had made that they would find him there in that area and sure enough, Walt Hamblin, who presently was the sheriff of Kane County, he jumped that wolf. He took in after him, and of course he had his rifle, but shooting from a horse, he wasn't doing very good. He run the wolf across a washboard place, solid stone, cross-bedded, where the sand had all blown off. And the wolf run across that and went around a projection, a little ledge, and there was the Paria Creek, which nothing could cross because it was 600, 700, and 1,000 feet deep. It was about 16 foot across and too wide for a wolf to jump so Walt Hamblin thought, "Well, I've got him now." And he went over there and got off his horse so he could get a better shot at him because he knew there was no way for the wolf to get away with this here tremendous gorge on one side and the ledge on the other. He kept approaching around the shelf slowly and he got there and, lo and behold he saw a bridge across this sixteen-foot span. Never knew it was there. And the wolf had gone across this bridge into the Escalante country and then the cattlemen over there began to lose their cattle.

It was resolved that this bridge was built by the Robbers Roost gang[43] because the cattlemen never could find where that gang had drifted cattle out of the country. They knew they stole them, they missed their cattle, but they never could find them. But no tracks showed on the cross-bedded sandstone, which is about five acres in extent there. I've been there. And, therefore, when the gang drifted the cattle through the sand, they'd drift them onto these rocks and no tracks would show. They drifted the cattle over there then they'd fallen these long cedars across the Paria Creek, and bound them together with rawhide and made a bridge, and they were over in a new country, isolated from all this other country by this tremendous Paria Creek gorge. And so that was how the Robbers Roost gang got the stolen cattle out of the country; they drifted them over to the Escalante country into Boulder and sold them. And no one knew it until this timber wolf event.

Buffalo Jones "Outbuffalos" a Buffalo

Now I want to tell you some buffalo stories. Buffalo Jones, who owned a buffalo herd, drifted those buffalo from Lund, Utah, in short, daily drifts to Jacob's Lake.[44] And I was there at Jacob's Lake the night the buffalo were corralled there in the Bar Z corrals. Buffalo Jones, as he was called, went out into the corral to look at the condition of these buffalo, and especially to inspect their hooves and so forth, to see whether he should continue on because the buffalo had become quite lame.

---

[43]Taylor Button's gang.

[44]According to an Arizona Game and Fish Department Bulletin entitled *Buffalo* (Form 4037, revised 9/70), Buffalo Jones shipped via railroad from Garden City, Kansas, to Lund, Utah, eighty-seven head of buffalo and trail-herded them 200 miles to the Kaibab Plateau, early in 1906. According to the bulletin, this shipment augmented a "nucleus herd" of thirty to forty head, which Jones had trail herded along the same route in July, 1905. Jones's purpose was to hybrid the buffalo with Galloway cattle which would be not only larger but would better be able to survive the desert conditions. His experiment was a failure, but remnants of the buffalo herd are maintained today by the Arizona Game and Fish Commission at House Rock.

Well, I had never seen a live buffalo before, but beyond that, the thing that sticks in my memory about this event was the fact that a buffalo bull attacked Buffalo Jones while he was out there, but instead of running, as I would have done, Buffalo Jones got right down on his hands and knees and with his hands he threw dirt just like the buffalo did. Jones just pawed and pawed the dirt and threw it high. The buffalo would swing one foot and then the other, and Jones would do the same and they came within six inches of each other with their heads and the buffalo backed away.

This was a great thing to watch, for me, because I didn't think any man living would dare go up against a big buffalo like that, a wild buffalo. But believe it or not, the buffalo gave up and backed away and Jones still pawed the dirt there. This little incident has always stuck in my mind as quite an event in my cowboy life.

"Darting" From A Buffalo

I had further experiences with the buffalo. Their range was the House Rock Valley. But one time I saw a lone bull up toward Crane Lake on the Kaibab. This was unusual and I wondered what he was doing up there. He was in a little swale and there was a little lake there. I thought, "Oh, boy, I'll go down and just take a good look

at him." I pulled off into this little valley where he was and, boy, he come at me like a bullet. The horse I was riding was named Dart and sometime prior to this time, when my brother was riding him, a maddened cow with sharp horns had gored this horse in the thigh, in the right hind leg, and Dart was very much concerned about such an event happening again. So with all his might, he raced with me on his back, and I leaned forward, giving him all the assistance I could. We outdistanced the buffalo so he didn't catch us.

Branding Buffalo

Later I had quite a bit of experience with the buffaloes, these buffalo herds. Along in about 1908 or '09 or '10 or '11 or '12, in that area, when I was associated with the buffalo, it was our duty as cowboys to brand the calves that were born to this herd. And I have gone down the rope after my good friend, Alec Indian, had roped one of these little, young buffalo calves, to see just how easy it was to handle a buffalo calf, to see whether he had more strength or more agility or was more vicious than a young, domesticated calf was. So I went down the rope on this occasion to throw this buffalo calf over my hip so that we might brand him, and I just couldn't do it. He threw me over his hip several times. Boy, he was strong. So it was necessary to pick up his hind legs with a lariat and stretch him out with the other horse, it was my horse, before we could brand him.

Old Cattalo

Incidentally, one of these buffalo cows became crossed with a white-faced Hereford Bar Z bull and the result was a "cattalo" which was quite notorious in the country. I also branded and castrated this cattalo, and years later the cowboys took him up to Jacob's Lake and they built a pen for him and fed him hay and Highpockets charged fifty cents apiece for tourists to see this white-spotted buffalo. He was just like a buffalo and cow, half cow and half buffalo. He was tall, really tall, and he created quite a sensation among the tourists there because they'd never had a cross between a buffalo and a Hereford as far as was known in that area of the country. And in Yellowstone Park, they'd never reported any such thing with the great herd they have there. So I had something to do, quite a serious operation, in fact, on this half-breed buffalo, Old Cattalo. I don't know what became of him, but I do know that they brought him to Kanab. They bought him from the Arizona government, the State of Arizona, and brought him to Kanab. And Al Drake, a pretty good cowboy and a very good bronco buster, tried to ride him at the Fourth of July celebration in the rodeo there and the cattalo threw him sky-high, threw Al Drake sky-high right there on the town square.

Lightning In The Forest

When I was eight years old, I was confirmed a member of The Church of Jesus Christ of Latter-day Saints. Sixty years later, I can vividly remember that confirmation and the promise that by keeping the commandments of God, I would always have a still, small voice to guide me and to protect me throughout my lifetime. This narrative reveals three instances, there have been many, in which this promise was literally fulfilled in my behalf.

I have always been an admirer of nature and the works of God in our universe and have humbly tried to understand them. I have witnessed, in my lifetime, with awe and admiration, and without fear,

quite a number of incidents relative to the elements obeying natural laws, such as cyclones, floods, violent blizzards, and lightning and thunder storms.

Many times, I have watched with pleasure but with awe exceptional thunder storms and sought a place of vantage in order to behold lightning displays, notwithstanding that three of my personal acquaintances have been killed by lightning.

In the summer of 1912 I was a cowboy on the Kaibab Forest, Arizona, and this particular day my uninteresting job, because it offered little excitement, was to graze the day herd. The herd was only about 150 head and my foreman thought one good cowhand was sufficient for the job. This day, however, proved to be one of excitement and one which often returns vividly to my mind. While grazing the day herd in the vicinity of Crane Lake, about midday, a violent thunder storm came up out of the southwest. The cattle took shelter on the lee side of clumps of quaking aspens and pine trees, but as usual, in order to get a better view as the storm approached, I rode my horse higher on the slope of the shallow glen where I was grazing my herd and stopped my horse under a tremendous ponderosa pine tree. From this point I could see the lightning display in the forest which increased with intensity as the storm crest came nearer. I saw the smoke break forth from a great pine tree on the opposite ridge and at that moment the still, small voice told me to move quickly from under my sheltering pine. My horse was most nervous and did not share my enjoyment of the storm. I touched him lightly with the spurs and he leaped into a gallop. Our destination was a small clump of quaking aspens about fifty yards distant. When about half way there, a simultaneous white flash and tremendous roar filled the immediate forest. At that instant, my horse tumbled to the ground, throwing me rolling in front of him and as I looked back, pieces of the pine tree which I had been under were flying through the air in all directions. My horse and I had been miraculously preserved.

Years later I took my wife and three children off the main highway to the Grand Canyon to see the place where this incident occurred and related the story to them. The shagged stump and the scattered pieces of the Monarch of the Forest still were in evidence.

In 1914 my good friend, Archie Swapp of Kanab, and I were hunting cattle near Dry Park in the Kaibab Forest. A violent thunder storm forced us to take shelter under the pine trees. The lightning was striking all around us and it seemed to us as if one place was as safe as another. Again the small voice seemed to tell me to move quickly. Archie didn't hear the voice at all. Without hesitation I gave spurs to my horse and shouted above the roar of the storm to my companion to follow and, as we reached the open valley, this same bright flash and simultaneous crash, which I had experienced at Crane Lake, resounded in our ears and our horses leaped faster forward. After we got about fifty yards away, we looked back over our shoulders and we witnessed the destruction of the great pine tree under which we had sought shelter. There wasn't a piece as big as your hat left anywhere. My friend afterwards realized that our lives were saved through my quick action and often asked how I knew that the lightning was going to strike that particular tree. "How'd you know to get out from under that tree?" he'd ask.

A number of years after this event, the Kaibab Forest Supervisor, Roach, and his wife and two small children, were my guests on an automobile trip from Kanab, Utah, to Bright Angel Point on the north rim of the Grand Canyon. Bright Angel is a distance of eighty miles from Kanab, but there were no surfaced roads in the area so our plans were to leave Kanab at daybreak and go to Bright Angel Point for a view of the Grand Canyon and to remain at this point for a basket lunch, then return to Jacob's Lake Ranger Station for the night and return to Kanab the following day. As there was very little travel in the area at that time, we did not anticipate seeing anyone except the forest ranger in charge of the Jacob's Lake Ranger Station. It was a beautiful summer day about the middle of July and we looked forward to a glorious ride through the virgin Kaibab Forest with its magnificent pines intermingled with quaking aspen groves. The children enjoyed watching the deer as they scampered through the forest at our approach. Occasionally we stopped to watch the antics of the white-tailed squirrels as they leaped from pine to pine.

While enjoying one of these stops, we noticed great thunderclouds approaching from the north and we decided that if we were to keep ahead of the storm and reach the safety of a partially-constructed ranger station at Bright Angel Point, it would be necessary to drive with all the speed the road would allow. Great shafts of lightning struck deep into the forest behind us and it was evident that a major storm was sweeping across the entire forest. Our thoughts were on our destination, and the beauty of the forest, with its draws and glades with the beautiful flowers, swept by unnoticed.

As we approached Bright Angel, we noticed great thunderheads making up over the canyon and this storm was coming from the south directly toward us. By the time we reached the end of the road, which ended at the rim of the canyon about fifty yards from the ranger cabin under construction, the storm in the canyon was a great sight to behold. My guests took the children and ran to the shelter of the cabin, but I was so thrilled with the awesome and furious storm raging down in the great chasms of the Colorado River, that I chose to sit in my car and watch the great, forked lightning bolts strike deep into the darkening gorge before me. It was the most unusual sight in my lifetime and one I had often hoped to see. The roar of the thunder reverberated from ledge to ledge without ceasing and actually seemed to shake the earth. Soon the crest of the storm hit the rim of the gorge and the rain came down in torrents. I was blinded by the lightning flashes but still chose to remain in my car which was partly under a small pine tree about five yards from the very edge of the canyon rim. I knew my companions were sheltered in the partially built cabin and I decided, from the intensity of the storm, that it would be of short duration and that I could remain dry sitting under the canvas top of the Buick.

At that moment, again, the still, small voice urged me to move quickly from the car. I dashed at full speed through the downpour toward the partly finished ranger station and my companions who had sought its shelter when we first arrived at the rim. I was possibly half way to my destination when a simultaneous blinding flash and roar seemed to shake the earth and atmosphere. Within seconds, I was upon the porch of the station and out of the downpour. Mrs. Roach, with her children clinging to her, was terribly frightened and her children were crying. The noise of the downpour on the roof of the cabin added to the vibrating impulses of the thunder as it rolled from ledge to ledge from the canyon below. Mr. Roach had never experienced such a storm, but was trying to quiet his wife and children. As I turned from this scene, I saw at about 100 yards distant, a gray jackass standing near a tremendous dead pine tree which stood in a small clearing of pine trees. At that moment I was blinded by a lightning flash and the earth shook again with the roar of the resulting thunder. When my eyes again regained their vision, the tremendous pine tree had disappeared and was laying in great broken pieces of smoldering wood. The jackass was sitting on its haunches like a big dog and remained so until the storm had passed. Then I urged him to get up and he sauntered off. Only a hole in the earth remained of the giant pine tree that formerly stood there. The tree under which I had parked my car had also been hit by the lightning and had split open, and the ignition wires of the engine had been burned.

Prospecting Without a Mule: Or, Tragedy in the Grand Canyon

This is a story about prospecting without a mule. As the owner and operator of a garage business in Kanab, Utah, in 1923, I became acquainted with all of the stockmen who had automobiles, some of whom had pickup trucks. On one occasion, I equipped one of my customer's trucks with a Moore transmission. This was a Ford car but with this transmission it gave it four speeds forward and it would climb almost anywhere a wagon had traveled. My customer's name was Nephi Johnson, a good friend who had been a cowboy south of the Grand Canyon in Arizona for quite a number of years. He had returned to Kanab and gone into the angora goat business and presently was owner of a large herd of these goats.

One day about the first of February, Windy Jim, a real prospector, made his initial appearance in Kanab with some very rich ore samples that he had procured along a shelf in the gorge of the Colorado River about seven miles east of where the old stockman's road came close to the rim, near the Mount Trumble Mountains. He interested the hotel manager, a very good friend of mine, in investing in the claim as he did also several other stockmen in the area. And they, in order to develop the prospect, had to build about seven miles of road up to the claim, and the claim was down under the top of the hanging ledge about four or five hundred feet and was on a fairly wide shelf. Now they got wagons, and several teams with scrapers, and men with shovels and they soon constructed this seven-mile road sufficient for an automobile truck to go up to the claim with supplies and working equipment and men.

About two weeks after the men had begun to work and to build equipment for the working of the claim, my friend, who owned the Ford pickup truck, the one on which I had previously installed a Moore transmission, came to me with a proposition. He said that he knew all that country down in that area across the Colorado gorge, across from where this Windy Jim claim was located, as he had been a cowboy there for quite a number of years, and if I would condescend to join him in a proposition, and help with the prospecting and also the financial part of the expedition, he would give me half interest in whatever we, together, found. I agreed upon this, and when we got his truck all equipped and went over to the Cattlemen's Equitable Store, the manager there said, "Where you going with all this equipment, with all these supplies?" And we told him it was a secret prospecting trip and we didn't want him to divulge the whereabouts of the location. And he said, "Well if you'll cut me in, I'll furnish all the supplies you need for one-third interest." So we agreed right there to do so. And we loaded up our truck. And I had previously told my wife we was going on this trip with Mr. Johnson for a few days and got her consent.

That afternoon we left Kanab on the old wagon trail to Lee's Ferry and arrived there just about sundown and employed the ferryman, Jerry Johnson, to cross our truck over on the ferry and deliver us to the south side of the Colorado River. We continued on from there to Peach Springs, Arizona, a country with which Mr. Johnson was well acquainted. And from Peach Springs we went over to a windmill pump about ten miles from there toward the Colorado River and from there it was necessary to go east somewhat and follow cattle trails until darkness overtook us and we made camp. The next morning, at sunrise, we were ready to travel by foot with a small pack and with a minimum quantity of clothing as we were hiking and we didn't want to be burdened with extra coats. So we stripped down to our shirts and proceeded to hike toward the south rim of the Colorado River, heading due north. As darkness came, we gathered enough wood to provide us warmth around the campfire through the long night.

As we approached our camping location, we noticed a great number of coyotes in the area, all of which were shy of man, of course, and a great many big jack rabbits who would spring out from their hiding place and dash away, leaping with their kangaroo leap to make observation as to where their pursuers were. As we finished our meager meal around the campfire and were preparing to stretch out nearby after gathering plenty of firewood, we noticed that a great many eyes were looking at us, and we determined, as we looked out from the campfire, that these were coyotes that had come to investigate the fire. And after darkness fell, we heard a great chorus of coyotes throughout the surrounding area where we were camped and apparently they were calling all of the coyotes to assemble and the assembly place was near our campfire. We were not particularly afraid of them, but we didn't have a gun as we were traveling light; we had left our .22 rifle with which we killed cottontails and other game, and therefore we couldn't frighten them off. As we supposed, they were frightened of the fire and would only come within about four rods. That'd be about fifty or sixty feet from the fire, but they circled the entire fire area and it was quite a thrilling experience to look in all directions and see the reflection of the fire in the eyes of all those coyotes. So it meant that each one of us would take an hour's sleep, then wake the other one who had been tending guard. In case that they did come closer, we could throw fire brands at them; we kept plenty of firewood on so that we could grab the unburned end and hurl it through the air at them had they approached. We got through the night that way and by daylight all of the coyotes had left and after a meager breakfast we again proceeded toward the south rim of the gorge of the Colorado River.

And we made it in about two hours' hike and determined from an observation point that the beginning of that newly-made road was a considerable distance west of where we had come to the rim. So we hurried back as fast as we could go on foot to our truck and then proceeded back to the mill and water and from there we followed the ore road which had been constructed from a mine that Mr. Johnson knew about. We got to a loading platform about noontime without any particular difficulty on the old road and we left our truck there; that was as far as it could be driven. Then we took our water canteen and a little bag of food supplies and headed out toward the east along the shelf which we knew the outcropping would be in if it coincided with the Windy Jim outcropping on the north side of the canyon.

We traveled until nighttime and hadn't arrived at the point we were hoping for. We found a cave which would accommodate both of us, barely, with enough shelf room in front of it, before dropping off the main ledge, to build a fire which would provide heat in the cave. We were sound asleep when a thunderstorm broke out and in a few minutes water was pouring down the channel leading to this cave. What didn't flow on over into the gorge came back around, followed the rock into the cave, and tried to wash us out of there. It swept our fire out immediately, of course, and all our wood we had stacked up. So it was necessary to lay there until daylight before we dared move. We were wet but sheltered from the wind so we didn't suffer too much. But it was daylight before we could see our way and be safe leaving that cave.

Going further up on the main shelf, we proceeded on eastward for about two hours and the going got quite rough and pretty hard to navigate. So we decided to go up on top of the main shelf at the first opportunity, which we did, and went up through a rockslide and went up on top and of course the terrain there was level and we made good headway afoot then. The same afternoon, just before sundown, we approached what we thought would be about straight across the gorge from the Windy Jim claim. And we looked over the ledge, and down on this wide shelf below us was this outcropping of a different character rock. It was mineralized and of course it was easily identifiable. And this was the point and the place that we had made this long trip to locate.

Johnson went east further to see if there was a possible chance of getting down through this upper ledge without going back to the place where we crawled out about noon. That was quite a long ways, and we knew that was the only place we could get down on that shelf. We had not seen any other break in the upper ledge. But right immediately in front of us was a tunnel that, looking down into, looked like it went clear down onto the ledge below, onto a shelf, not a very wide shelf but a shelf about half way down to the shelf that we wanted to travel on where the outcropping was. And so while Johnson went east to investigate some other entrance to that shelf, I went down through this tunnel in the ledge, and, by using my knees and hands and hanging onto rock projections, I got down to the little seven-foot-wide shelf which appeared from the top of the ledge to blend in as it went westward onto the main shelf. This is what I hoped it would do. And so I went to the end of it–about 150 yards–and it lacked about fifty feet of reaching the upper edge of the shelf on which we wanted to work. And I decided that was the end of my journey there so I retraced my steps and got halfway up through the end of the tunnel and met my partner coming down.

Johnson was stuck there in the tunnel in a narrow place and I tried to lift him out by letting him put his feet on my shoulders. It was difficult for me to hang on with my elbows and my knees and my feet and I couldn't push him back up through; he'd got wedged in there. So we decided to pull him on down through and go out on that shelf and take a twenty-five foot, quarter-inch sea grass rope, which I had wound around my waist, and anchor it on the end of that shelf and slide down it and drop off it onto the shelf below.

We made a small loop in the end of the rope and hooked it over a stable rock, part of the shelf. I slid down first to the knot at the end, then I hung by my hands and swung out a little so I would miss a big boulder immediately under me and I hit the soft talus down there just like a cushion. Then I removed all the rocks, this rock and the other rocks nearby, out of the sand, so that when Mr. Johnson came down he wouldn't be injured. So I shouted up to him to throw down our food and canteen, and he come down the rope and hung onto the knot as long as he could, then he let go and he plowed out the sand for quite a little distance there as it sloped off toward the main shelf. We gathered up our canteen and our food bag and headed around the shelf toward the claim.

We got about 100 yards from there and, crouched over in a little niche in the ledge, was a magnificent mountain sheep. He was a beautiful specimen; he stood there a-stomping his feet and making the dust fly as he stomped and he dared anyone to come near him. Mr. Johnson was rushing on around to the claim and I said, "Come on back here and see this beautiful mountain sheep." He said, "The hell with the mountain sheep, let's get some beautiful mountain ore." And he was gone, so I followed him and paid no more attention to the sheep except to make sure he didn't attack me with those tremendous curled horns.

I caught up to Mr. Johnson at the outcropping, and oh, it was a beautiful sight with quartzite and crystals and quite an area of mineralized ore. And so we proceeded to build monuments, stake them out according to the law. We had procured at Flagstaff, Arizona, from the county there, prospector's claim forms, and we filled out one of these claim forms and buried it in a can which formerly had contained part of our grub, some pork and beans. And we built this right into the monument the next morning. But first, we gathered firewood to keep us warm in that cave.

We hadn't explored the cave until this point and so we carried the firewood to the mouth of the cave. By this time it was dark and we lighted the fire and, lo and behold, we about lost our buttons. This entire cave, as big as the interior of a good-sized room in a home, literally sparkled like diamonds, every square inch was a diamond, and it almost blinded us to look at the reflection from our fire as we looked inward from the cave entrance. So we thought we were living in heaven that night. We laid down by the fire to keep warm and in the morning we got up and built our monuments and ate the last parcel of our food that we had brought with us. Then we chipped off broken pieces of the samples of the rock and wrapped all of the samples, the choicest ones at least, in one of our red bandanas from around our necks.

And we proceeded back on that shelf to see if we could retrieve the rope that was hanging from the ledge above. And we threw rocks at that little loop up there about fifty feet away until our arms gave out and we decided it was hopeless to try and recover that rope. We didn't know whether we'd need it again or not, but we would've liked to have recovered it. Then we walked westward, intending to crawl off of this ledge at the place we had crawled out at noon the day before and get up on top where it would be easy going. But as we did so, the shelf began to narrow markedly. We did find a fresh water spring, however, coming out of the ledge and we refilled our canteen and had a good drink. Then we went about 150 yards and the ledge terminated in a gorge that reached clear, almost, to the bottom of the canyon, four or five hundred feet straight down, perpendicular, with a gap of about ten feet to the shelf beyond.

Now we drew cuts here to see who would run and jump first. And Johnson got the short stake; that meant he ran first and jumped. So we threw the canteen of water over across on the shelf and also the handkerchief with our samples in it, well beyond where we would land when we would reach there with our feet. It was a little difficult to run straight, you had to run a little bit on an arc. So Johnson got back about twenty-five yards and ran and he jumped, but as he landed, he hit the overhanging ledge with the left side of his head just above his temple, and of course he was immobilized immediately. He laid stretched out there on the ledge without even moving for several minutes, and it seemed like several hours to me, and all the time I was shouting, "Double up your knees, Neph, double up your knees." So when he did regain consciousness he heard me, as he said afterward, and he pulled his knees up under him, 'cause his feet were hanging out over the ledge, and had he rolled the wrong way, he'd a gone down, a way down, and we never would have recovered his body. And then as he regained consciousness, he crawled out along the ledge, then out of my way, so that I ran and jumped and made a more successful jump because as I landed I crouched low and did not hit the overhanging part of the ledge as he had done.

And so then I took my bandana handkerchief from my neck, dumped out the ore samples on the ledge, then wet the handkerchief with the cold water from the canteen and bathed his wounded head with it for a little while until he got his senses back. Then we wrapped his head up with the two bandanas, the wet one over the wound and the dry one to hold it in place under his hat as we proceeded toward our car. He could not walk straight and it was necessary for me to hold him all the time by one arm and we made the rock slide, which was our destination, and we climbed out of this up on top. From there it was not difficult traveling and I led him back to our car and we got back to it about two hours before sundown. I prepared a good meal, we had plenty of food there, prepared a good meal while he bathed his head with the cold bandanas to ease the pain.

And we took the old road back to the windmill where we replenished the water in our canteen and rested a few minutes. Then we bathed Neph's head with the wet bandana and tied it on so it would be effective while we rode along in our truck toward Peach Springs. From there we went to Harper's Ferry and ferried across the Colorado River on to Las Vegas where the doctor told us we had done everything we could do under the circumstances. We continued on to St. George where we had some minor mechanical trouble repaired at the garage and then continued on to Hurricane by way of the Virgin River highway and then on to Pipe Springs and over through Fredonia to Kanab where I delivered Neph to his family.

They consulted the local doctor and he determined that it would be better to drive Neph to Panguitch for consultation with the doctor there. Then they went on to Salt Lake City where he received some attention. He then was returned to Kanab where he passed away in just a very short time.

While he was confined at Kanab, Dr. Mayo, of the Mayo Clinic, came to my garage for service and for some road information. I became acquainted with him sufficient to ask if he would do me a favor and he replied in the affirmative and I told him about this prospecting trip and my injured partner. And he said he would accompany me to his home and make an examination. And it was from his examination that the family took him to Salt Lake, the trip previously spoken of.

So this was the end of a rather dramatic, non-profitable prospecting expedition triggered by a total stranger to the community, the prospector by the name of Windy Jim and his famous mine.

Part Four

"Fording" along in Our Model T's

Charlie McCornick

Well, there was only four of us in Kanab that had automobiles, and I had one. So if anything went wrong with the other three, they'd always come to me because they thought I knew something about them. And I did—a little, very little. So then I had to fix them. Well, we were sitting down to the post office on our boots one morning, whittling, waiting for the stage to come in, you know.

And we looked down to the corner and we heard somebody talking, and Charlie McCornick was coming around talking out loud to himself. He'd walked four miles in those high-heeled boots, you know, and he was pretty mad. And I said, "What's the matter, Charlie?" And he said between swear words (he could profane more than any man in this world that I have ever heard and I have heard some pretty profane speakers, you know, when they get mad on the range sometimes)—well, between swear words, which was three or four swear words to each intelligible word, he said, "I was coming up the hill down at the halfway place and she wouldn't take it in high and I socked her into intermedium and the transom fell out." He meant the transmission. He called it the intermedium, you know. He didn't know the difference in those days. So that's one of my choice stories about him.

Orange Juice

I was one of the very first people to drive to the Grand Canyon in a car. And, by the way, I've driven a lot of those roads. The one that goes into House Rock Valley, I was the first one to drive that. I was the first one to drive the North Kaibab road down into Coyote; I drove the very first car that ever traveled either of those roads. I was the first one to go into the House Rock Valley down toward Kane and the first car to drive to Bright Angel Point; isn't that something?

We had these Fords, you know, and the gas tank was up under the seat. If you got on a steep hill, the gas tank wouldn't feed to the carburetor, so we'd have to turn around and back up the hill. And then we'd all jump in and coast down.

One time we had a crate of oranges with us and the roads used to be just wagon roads. We had the oranges on the running board and every once in a while this board on the bottom of the crate broke off. The brush had broke off one little slat, you know. And every little while an orange would drop down in that rut and the hind wheel would get it—we didn't know what was doing all this popping and finally we stopped and got out and there was the last orange. Wouldn't you have known, twenty dollars a crate. They was the only oranges in Kanab and they'd just got in by freight. Took them three weeks from Marysvale to get them down there. They was the first ones that summer to come from Los Angeles.

Honeymooning On The Arrowhead Trail

On June 5, 1917, in the St. George Temple, I married Romania Fawcett of St. George. We took a honeymoon trip to Los Angeles by way of stage and train to visit my sister, Jane Townsend. After a couple of weeks in that vicinity, I purchased a stripped-down, custom-made Model T Ford. It had bucket seats and a canvas top, twenty-gallon gasoline tank, small running boards from fender to fender on each side for carrying luggage, and it also had a tool chest back of some bucket seats on the chassis. The man who had built this for his own private use was inducted into the service and therefore I got a good buy on it.

We left L.A. at daylight one morning to go home on the recently established Arrowhead Trail, which at that time went by way of Riverside and then to San Berdino,[45] then over Cajon Pass by way of Victorville, then followed the railroad eastward toward Needles on the Colorado River. At Goff's it turned north toward Las Vegas by way of Searchlight. The road was just a wagon road and the gauge of the automobiles in those days was different so the wheels missed by four inches; only two wheels would fit in the groove and the other two had to go on top of the sand so you rode cockeyed. The trail was marked by a few signs where you made right-angled turns and they had pasteboard signs up and an arrow showing where to turn at that point.

Our first day, including part of the night, we had considerable trouble due to high pressured tires (which were used in those days)

---

[45]San Bernardino.

taking on extra pressure as we mounted the mountain at Cajon Pass where we had several blowouts before I knew what the trouble was. I supposed the tires were just old. But the high pressure, due to elevation and high temperature, blew them out. Although we had two extra tires, it required putting tubes in them and blowing them up with a hand pump which was time consuming and, under the heat of the day, was rather exhausting, plus I got blisters on my feet through my shoes from standing in the scorching sand.

There were no motels in those days, so we thought we'd travel to a little hotel at a railroad stop at Thermo where they took on water for the steam engines. A few miles before we got to this point, we caught up to a little car. The driver and his wife asked us to stay with them in the desert. The woman asked my wife to sleep with her in a bed they made up in the car and the men slept on a tarpaulin in the sand. But this woman had a little dog which licked my wife's face, so Romania came over and took my hand and we quietly took off across the desert to Goff's. And a railroad crew there invited us to have breakfast; very fine food and we enjoyed it. We filled up our water canteen, then drifted north toward Searchlight and the hot desert.

Soon after we left Searchlight, it became dark and, as we turned out to let another car pass us, we got stuck because we were out of the wagon-road tracks. The people in the other car were afraid to travel along at night, so we laid down in the sand together till daylight and they helped push us back into the tracks again and we went on toward Las Vegas, arriving there about ten o'clock in the morning. There was a hotel there but they had no accommodations so we decided to go on toward St. Thomas (a town which is now under Lake Mead) which was approached through the Valley of Fire, a very colorful formation in the earth's surface.

When we got to St. Thomas, we got some refreshments, grocery supplies to carry with us, and we decided to go on toward our destination in St. George by way of Mesquite, the crossing point of the Arrowhead Trail over the Virgin River. At that point the town had furnished a man with a team of horses to pull travelers across the treacherous quicksand of the river which was several hundred yards wide at that point. We didn't know he was stationed there until we were half away across and we heard a shout of warning behind us and here he came, dashing along behind us with his team of horses, riding one of them, and we waved at him and thanked him for his good efforts but we made it on our own.

We got into Bunkerville and then went on up the river across the bench land to Littleton which was the turn-off point to go over Mormon Hill toward Santa Clara and our destination, St. George. When we got into the Santa Clara Creek just below the Mormon Hill, we found it was necessary to cross that small stream seventeen times in order to get to the town of Santa Clara. Without stopping there we proceeded on four or five miles to St. George and arrived there at four o'clock in the morning. Romania's mother put us to bed and let us sleep for twenty-four hours without disturbing us. She thought we were dead.

We stayed there several days getting our tires repaired before proceeding up the Virgin River, which also had to be crossed or forded, to Hurricane, and from there we went up the steep Hurricane Hill and made Kanab in a drive of twenty-four hours from the time we left St. George.

Every year since that time, except for the last two years, I have traveled over that Arrowhead Trail to Los Angeles and have marveled at the improvements made year by year. It is my desire now to go down through the Virgin River Gorge to the town of Littlefield instead of going over Mormon Hill. That road is almost completed and I hope to drive it this fall.[46]

That's the end of my honeymoon trip. We only saw two cars on the entire trip—one whose woman occupant offered my wife her bed at the railroad stop and the other people where we got stuck when we turned out for them as they were going toward Goff's and we were headed for Searchlight and we laid down on the canvas for a few hours with them and watched the stars.[47]

---

[46]1973.

[47]The following interchange between Rider and his wife, Romania, adds a few more interesting details of this trip:

Romania: We were one of the first to come from Los Angeles on the Arrowhead Trail. That was June, 1917. That was a nightmare; three days and three nights. Oh, that was terrible. We thought we was going to die but we didn't. We had to pawn our rings and our watches and everything.

Rider: We didn't have any tires. Our tires would go like those oranges; one tire would pop and then in a little while another one would pop. You know, they had

Washout

One time Grandmother, me and Ramona, who was just a baby, were going to St. George from Kanab and the weather was fine, but there was a big thundercloud up above, down toward Gould's ranch, and the road went in a wash for about six miles and no way out. So we entered this wash and it was perfectly dry. It looked fine. But all of a sudden—we saw this big cloud up there and thunder and lightning—and all of a sudden, the water began to come in every little wash all down there. Finally, it got to floating us along. It got so deep we couldn't get out. So I had Grandma get ready. I said, "Now, you get out, and you get on that bank, and you run along, and when I get down here a ways on that next turn, where it makes a turn, I'll be over close to you, and I'll toss the baby out." And she caught her.

Well, I grabbed hold of the steering wheel and I went on down. Finally, down there where the road left the wash, it turned at right angles, and lucky there was a place like that because as the water turned at right angles, why, I was going so danged fast, I went right up this slope where they'd excavated to let the wagons out, you know. And that put the carburetor up out of water; so I got under there and drained it and cranked it and away I went, and pulled on out, and we got into St. George that night about midnight.

Mohair

Grandmother and I was coming from Salt Lake and we met Charlie Cram—he was trucking mohair to the railroad at Marysvale—who was parked along the road. And he had way up on top of his

---

those hard tires and no roads, and the heat of the desert expanded them so they'd just blow out.

Romania: When we go to Los Angeles now we laugh about that trip. Good thing we was on our honeymoon or we never could have stood it.

Rider: Changing tires—the sand was so hot it blistered my feet and then I couldn't wear my shoes at all.

Romania: The wind blew the sand and it'd just hit your face. I had to wear a veil just tied real tight around my face.

Rider: That sand would blow along and take all the paint off the car. You wouldn't have anything, it was just raw iron left.

truck these big sacks of mohair as long as the truck bed is wide. We stopped there and said hello to him and I got out of the car and said, "Charlie, did you know you have a left hind wheel down here?" And he says, "I have?" And he gave another pull on his cinch rope and he cut the rope in half and he keeled over, just a perfect somersault, and lit on his feet and he says, "Which one, which one?" And I says, "that one right there." And he said, "That isn't flat." And I said, "I didn't say it was. I just said, did you know you had a rear hind wheel?"

Part Five

Stories of Kanab, Utah

Youth: Of Toys, Toes, and Indians

I was born in Kanab, down on the Arizona border. It's a beautiful town in the red hills. My first recollections are of having bone horses and cattle and sheep which we would keep in the little corrals we made by hand, little posts we would stick in the sand. These bone animals were made from the Pasturin joint of horses or cows, which extends from the ankle down to the hoof, and these joints look just like a horse almost, so we would paint them. My brother would bring them in off of the range and they would be as white as snow, you know, bleached in the sun, and we would put bridles on them and saddles on them made of string. And then we'd tie them to the post just like our brothers would do with their horses. They were quite important; that's the only toys we had.

But the Indians would steal over the fence and would come and steal these precious animals from us, out of our tents and out of our pastures, and therefore we would take after them with a bow and arrow, and we'd have a great time shouting and shooting them with our bows and arrows. And then sometimes my brother would put me on back of his saddle and we'd go uptown, and if we'd see any

Indians, he'd take after them and give a few war whoops and run them through the fence. So that's my recollection of the Indians in my early childhood up to the time I was six years old. My father, by the way, was ordained a bishop to the Lamanites by Brigham Young and was called to settle Kanab with some five other families that settled down there. And that's how I happen to be able to talk Indian. My father's name in the Piute tribe was *Pagamatoots* which means "Long Beard." He had a long beard, you know, clear down to here. And my name is *Pagamatoots Unis*—"Little Long Beard."

Well, anyway, none of the children down there had shoes. Our parents usually did, as I recall, but none of us did, not a single one of us in that town had shoes to wear. And on Sundays, they had a church bell up there in the tower in an old schoolhouse, and a guy would ring that and we could hear that peal all over town, and we'd all get to Sunday School. And so we would go with our sisters and brothers from our end of town to see how many of those kids up in the north end of town had web feet. And this is a fact; there was one family down there that had web feet.[48]

But in Sunday School the wood floor had a lot of knot holes in it, and the little mice would stick their heads out and their little beady eyes and whiskers, and I'd curl up my toes like this and crowd over to my sister, you know, 'cause I was afraid of those mice. Instead of looking for webbed feet I was looking for beady-eyed mice.

Pass the Butter, "Amen"

I was on horseback. I was coming out of Escalante to Kanab and I got in late at night and I saw this barn there. I knew that it would be all right if I fed my horse out of that barn hay and camped there at night. There were no hotels, you know, and, if I paid for using the barn the next morning, it would be fine and I could go on my way.

Well, anyway, I got up early and just got my fire going to cook my breakfast and Elijah Moore (we called him "Lige") come out there. He was the owner. He says, "What are you doing here?" And I said, "Well, I took my horses in there and fed them," and started

[48]Jacob Hamblin's family.

to feeling my pocket, getting my money, had a little old bag of gold, you know. I told him who I was and he said, "You Dave Rider's brother?" And I said, "Yes." My golly, he kicked that fire out that quick with his boot and he said, "You come right in the house. We are going to have breakfast right away, in a little while." but I said, "No, I don't want to bother your wife." I said, "I've got plenty of stuff here. I'll cook me something to eat." He said, "You aren't going to cook around my place. You come in."

He had three boys. I can't quite recall their names right now, three boys and two girls. And I could smell breakfast cooking. He said, "There's a wash basin." It was out on a porch outside. And all the other kids came out there, and they were washing and wiping their faces dry, you know. Hungry as the devil like kids get. They could smell this bacon. So by the time we all got washed and stood around that table to kneel down at the chair, it took us quite a while to get in there, but Moore wasn't going to kneel down until they all got there, and he counted them out and they were all there. So he did the praying and he prayed for everybody in the town, prayed for Joe Pollock who had a broken leg because he hit his horse over the head with a club and his horse kicked him and broke his leg. And I thought he was going to name everybody including myself. But anyway, I was about to die, you know, when all of a sudden he ended the prayer with, "Ma, the bread's burning, pass the butter, Amen!", all in one breath.

Flu Epidemic of 1918

When I got out of the army in November 1918, I had to come to St. George to get Romania and Ramona, who was then just three months old. When we got to Fredonia, why they had a chain across the Kanab Creek Bridge. It was just a narrow bridge (they've got a beautiful highway now), and they had a chain across and an armed guard out there. No one could enter that town. Ramona was crying, and it was cold, and it was in the night, and this guy had drove back to town to talk to the city board, council, whoever it was. "No, you can't come in here and don't you get within twenty yards." And he'd stand over there on that side of the bridge and we'd argue. The chain was there and that's as close as he dared come. So I says,

"Well, I'm coming through." I knew the guy well and I says, "I'm coming through, Olin." And he said, "Over my dead body you are." And I said, "You go back and talk." And Ramona started to cry and she cried so hard that he let us come over. He unlocked the chain and I went through and went on through town.

When I got up south of Kanab, down there at halfway place where this transom incident took place, you know, why, there was a tent with a light in it and a chain across the road. But luckily the chain wasn't confined to a bridge, so I just darted out through the sagebrush and went right on by. It was our neighbor next door, across the street, had a beautiful home, who was the guard in the tent. And, golly, they was going to put me in jail and everything else when they found out I got in town—and yet I was the only man that would take food to them and bury their dead. It was a good thing I was there. They had the roads barred north and south of Kanab and nobody could get in or out. Nobody would deliver any food. No store opened. Wouldn't let anyone in their stores. They were frightened to even talk to each other. Scared to death.[49]

Some Indians and I would bury all those people that died. The Indians, Jets Joe, Old Mose, Bullets, and Henry, were frightened; they wouldn't go near people that were sick. But they would dig the graves for me. We'd cart the dead by people's homes, and the fellows would be getting well. But they'd look out and see me going down with this wooden box and they knew I was going to the cemetery. By golly, they'd keel over, too. Healthiest men in the town. The very strongest men died.

Betting in Kanab

I wired all the homes in Kanab, except one, and that was the home of George Adams, who said that when they turned the switch on when the power plant was ready that every house in town would burn up. And my good friend, Gid Findlay, bet him a twenty-dollar

[49]Romania adds, "We had a doctor's certificate saying that we were all right or we never would have come. My doctor in St. George gave us a certificate but, of course, they were scared to death of it [the flu] but it finally got Kanab, but we didn't bring it to them. Somebody from the north came down."

gold piece that not a home would burn up. And when the switch was turned by my daughter, Ramona, and all the lights went on, my good friend, Gid Findlay, who always bet on me, collected the forty dollars that John Cram (we called him Highpockets, he was six foot six and a good cowboy) held; he was the stake holder. I saw him pay Gid Findlay two twenty-dollar gold pieces.

In those days there was no bank in Kanab, and everyone had gold and they kept it in buckskin bags about twice the size of a Bull Durham tobacco bag with a string zipper at one end to close the end off. In 1926, when I collected for the wiring of one man's home, for putting the electrical wiring in it and the outlets and the chandeliers, he took a twenty-dollar gold piece out of a bag like I described, and it was full. He had been a cattleman many years and was very conservative and that bag was his bank. He paid all his bills from it and no one robbed anyone in that area. The only robbery was when people bet that something could or could not be done, and that was the way they exchanged money from one hand to another.

They would bet on practically anything, how much a man weighed or whether one could wrestle a man down, or on a foot race or a horse race—oh, they bet lots on horse races—and they would bet on a hop, skip, and a jump, how far and who would be the winner in that contest. A good friend of mine, who has long since passed away, Homer Spencer, would always win and yet people would bet that sometime he wouldn't win and that someone else would beat him, you know. Outside of whittling down at the post office, waiting for the stage to come in, this was one of the unique and pleasant pastimes—to watch the betters, to see the bets made and see the stake holder pay the winner off. This was quite an affair in Kanab.

And they had rodeos in which they did the old-time method of roping a big steer and tying it. One cowboy on horseback had to do this and he would rope the steer and try to catch it by the horns by running directly back of it. And after he had secured the rope on the horns, then he would run on by the steer at full speed and as he went on by, the steer would naturally turn to the right and the cowboy would go to the left, going really in opposite directions, pulling the sixty-foot lariat tight. And, of course, the steer would go end over end and the cowboy would have to leave his horse and run back with his hog rope, tie one hind foot and two front feet of the steer together, before he'd throw up his hands for the judge to time him.

And that was a very interesting event. Everybody in town, of course, stood around the public square, which was fenced with a picket fence, and the perimeter was quite large and it afforded room for everyone to see the roping events. Side bets were placed by everybody, even kids would bet pennies, but the main prize, which went to the winner of the event, was usually a new saddle.

On one particular day the cowboys were sitting on the empty gas tanks in front of my garage. They were empty because we had to haul the gas in tanks from Marysvale, 130 miles by wagon, and unload them on the ground, then siphon the gasoline out into the gas tank below the pumps. And the cowboys sometimes would collect there and bring their sticks along to whittle. I had previously gone out to the city of Ryan, the old vacated city of Ryan, at which site the Coconina Copper Company had built a mill to process the copper-ore claims from the Jacob's Lake area. The mill had been abandoned because it cost too much to process the ore and haul the refined copper to the railroad at Marysvale, which was two hundred and some odd miles away from Ryan over bad wagon roads. And I had picked up some lead pipe that had been used in construction of this mill, and I took a conveyor belt bucket, as there were plenty of them laying around the mill site, and built a big fire and put this bucket on the coals and put these lead pieces in to melt them into a solid ingot which weighed about fifty pounds.

I had this ingot at my garage, and this particular day I brought it out and was showing it to some of the cowboys that were sitting around on the empty gas barrels whittling. And Highpockets, John Cram, who incidentally happened to always bet against me whenever anyone was betting for me, came down the street toward us and I said, "Here's a good chance for your bets, cowboys; I'm going to hand this to Highpockets and let him guess how much it weighs."

I could hold that ingot in one hand. It was V-shaped so I could take the top of the V and clinch it with my thumb and fingers and I lifted it up and handed it to him that way. I was very strong and I tried not to show my exertion at holding this thing out. As I handed it to him, he placed both hands under it, and I let it go, and it flipped him in half almost as he went clear to the ground to keep it from falling on his boots. He just doubled up when I dropped it in his hand. I'll never forget that. And they all got a big laugh out of that. So they asked him how much it weighed. So Cram picked it up, shook it a time or two, and said, "It weighs exactly fifty pounds."

But everyone didn't agree with that. They bet it didn't. And Cram would take their bets, you know, for he was wealthy. He'd take whoever wanted to bet that it didn't weigh fifty pounds. Well, sure enough, after all the bets were in and the stake holders had been selected, there must have been $150 or $200 bet on the weight of that ingot. They took it down to the post office and had Mr. Dalley, the postmaster at that time in Kanab, weigh it on the United States scales. I don't remember the weight of it exactly, but Highpockets, John Cram, did win. He got a lot of money, whatever the weight was. He won. He must of had a couple hundred in gold. The stake holders paid him off.

Carving the Cornerstone

The town of Kanab, prior to 1924, had had as a meeting house sort of a recreation hall built of lumber. But in 1924 they decided to build a ward chapel out of native materials including hand-kilned brick and hand-sawed and milled lumber from the Kaibab Forest. So this was a great undertaking for members of the Church in that area. And it was decided that this building should have a cornerstone as all of the Church buildings from the early days do. And into these cornerstones it has been the custom to put a sealed iron box with certain items of historical importance at the time of construction and to identify the men who contributed to the building of the structure.

Men had made trips around the area to see if they could procure a suitable stone for this purpose, but all of the available stones that had been looked at were not practical to square up and engrave. Therefore Bishop McCallister took with him a good cowhand, Brigham Riggs, to go look. They took provisions (hay and grain for their team and two saddle horses) and went into the Kanab Gorge by way of Hacks Canyon, the only canyon this side of the Grand Canyon that goes down into Kanab Creek Gorge. At the head of that canyon, because it was so steep and narrow, they dropped the back two wheels of the wagon, put a bar across the breach so it wouldn't tip on the axle, and wired it down. Then they proceeded with these two front wheels down into the gorge for several miles and, when it was impossible to take the two wheels any further, they dropped their grain and hay and they took their team with their harnesses on and their two saddle horses and went further down into what we call the Marble down there. They had to find a stone which had to be finished two courses high and two and a half courses long (about twenty by thirty inches, including the mortar), so this would have to be a stone that weighed about 1,100 pounds when completed. And they found one that they figured, after squaring up, would be large enough for the requirements of the cornerstone.

It was necessary to pry this stone loose, so they put their chains around it and then they put one horse of the team in front of the other, the chain right between his legs. And those horses dragged that stone up that way until they got back to the two wheels and then they got it rolled up on there, sort of snaked it up onto the platform of the front wheels. Then they proceeded with the team of horses to drag it up the rugged trail, up Hacks Canyon, to where they had left the running boards and hind wheels of the wagon. They had a wonderful team, a big, stout team. Well, anyway, from then on it was no trouble because they had it on a four-wheeled wagon and had a fairly good wagon road over into Kanab.

In the meantime, it was thought at Kanab that they had had difficulty because they had been gone so long–in fact the entire trip

took them three weeks—and they sent a cowboy rider, Ensign Riggs, Brig Rigg's son, to follow their trail to see what had happened to them. He found them just after they had loaded the stone on all four wheels of the wagon and were ready to proceed to Kanab, so he galloped ahead and come back into Kanab and told them, "Yes, they're all right."

Well, anyway, they got this stone to Kanab and then they didn't know what to do with it because it had to be all squared up. So I told them to take this rock to the backyard of my garage and I told them that I would square it up for them. I got a crosscut saw, the kind usually propelled by two men, one at each end, from the Forest Service supervisor whom I knew well, and he donated this saw to me to make a rectangular block out of this marble stone. But to do so, I had to take a Model T Ford and jack up one hind wheel and prepare a pitman upon that wheel by bolting a block of two-by-fours to it and I put a journal to it so that, as the wheel turned, it would oscillate the saw back and forth across this marble slab. The saw was positioned by parallel bars driven into the ground so that it would remain perfectly parallel and upright so it sawed right through the rock, just like you saw timber.

This stone had been the subject of great interest to the people of Kanab, but by word of mouth, it became of interest to all the people of the Kanab Stake including Alton, Glendale, Orderville, and Mt. Carmel and to the residents of Johnson Canyon. Many people came to watch and donate their time to pour water over the stone to keep it cool and wash out the saw of particles. And they'd pour sand in there, too, so the saw would cut, because the teeth wore off right away, you know, and after all these long teeth on that two-way saw had gone, they still would pour sand and water on and that saw would cut. Of course, I knew it would do that. So everybody in the county poured sand and water; the whole county was interested in that stone. Then we got it slabbed up; we had to saw the ends off the exact length, then we turned it flatways and sawed the top and the bottom flat, at right angles. But then the one end and the one side had to be polished and a lot of people worked on polishing. Oh, they brought carpet and they put sand on and Bon Ami (some of them thought it would be all right), and everybody'd get in there and take their exercise, then someone else would take over. They made a beautiful polish out of it.

This process continued about a week. And so then, after the stone was all squared up, they had to dig a hole in the middle of the top edge to put the metal box in that was to be sealed with all of the records of the contributors to the chapel and the history of how it was done. (By the way, I did the plumbing, heating and electrical wiring. And I also put the fountain in and the baptismal font and the boiler and heater.) But when Brig Riggs, this fellow that dug the stone out, and his son Delbert Riggs, both fine chiselers, got chiseling down into the top of this rock to seal up the metal box, they broke a little end out over there as it was a fragile rock, all right, and oh, everybody felt bad and I said, "Well, we'll make a little stone and fit it in that corner and put it in separately." It was the only thing we could do then. Oh, gee, we was sick about that. So was Brig Riggs; he'd just hammered down in there as they'd loosened the end and cracked it out. So we found out the rock was friable and also had flaws in it.

Well, it finally was ready to be engraved. The president of the stake had contracted with Elias Morris and Sons, monument cutters in Salt Lake City, to send two men down with their equipment to engrave this beautiful stone. It was now highly polished and there was a very beautiful picture displayed on one end and one side, with forests in the background, it seemed like, and stars in the heavens—and a number of flaws which were a difficult problem when it came to engraving. These men came from Salt Lake and stayed at the Hotel Rust. They had to bring their own equipment, including their own compressor, so they brought their truck. It took them two days to come to Kanab and it was late when they got to the hotel so they didn't look at the stone until the next morning. Then they looked at it and they looked at some of the pieces of the stone, the end pieces that we'd sawed off that were laying out there, and they examined them and they hammered on them a little and they looked the surface over and one thing and another. Said they'd spoil the stone if they did anything, so they put their tools in their truck and went back to Salt Lake City. I don't know what their fee was, but it was quite a bit.

All the local men were standing around to see the engraving, but the Salt Lake men filled their gas tanks at my garage and left. I said, "Good night, I don't know why they came all the way down here to do this job and then not do it. Any cowboy with any sense could carve that stone." And that was just a reflex action. I didn't know I was going to say it, but quite a few people heard me. No one said anything to me, but it wasn't a half hour and here the building committee and the president of the stake was up there and wanted to know if I made that statement. I couldn't lie out of it. I looked at the men standing around and I said, "I guess I must have or you wouldn't have come up here!" They said, "Can you do it?" And I said, "Sure. I'll tell you what I'll do. You get George Shield's blacksmith shop, where I won't be bothered, and get a man that will stay with me to keep the fire going and the lanterns going at night, and get someone to do his chores and my chores, and I'll do this stone for you and have it ready by ten o'clock next Saturday morning (which was only two and a half days away)." See, we only had forty-eight hours to do it; Melvin Ballard, apostle of the Latter-day Saint Church, would be there to dedicate and lay the stone.

So Jody Johnson (still a good friend whom I met and knew at Lee's Ferry), they got him and told him to come and help me. They got someone to do my chores and milk my cows and tend my horses, and they got somebody to do his, and his wife and my wife would bring our meals to us and put them through a little hole which was in the blacksmith shop. (I grew tired of looking at that window.) We had the door barred from the inside so no one could get in, and I really worked. I remember well how people would knock on the big front doors and we wouldn't let them in. We didn't have time, I said. "We've got this work to do. We've got to get this out of here."

All Jody had to do was to keep me company, you know, and when I sharpened my chisel, he'd have to turn a little hand grinder. We had to grind it by hand. That's all he had to do, but he was good company. I'd have gone to sleep the second day if it hadn't been for him, but he'd talk to me and keep me going. I was afraid that I would make a mistake and spoil the corners and the letters. Well, anyway, I practiced on the end of the stone first. I put the design on it, and then I turned the stone up so I could work. Jody and I tipped it up on carpet so we wouldn't break it. We were afraid of it after Brig Riggs had broken that corner out. We turned it up on the end and I put 1924 on the end I laid those letters out and they came out perfect. Boy, they looked good. Then we laid it down on the carpet there so I could do the face, and I laid out this big design, with the stars in each crest out at the end.

And I chiseled every letter on that design, put the big stars on there, the big circle up there, and on the face I put the "LDS Chapel." And I never broke a corner and there's two hundred and fifty some odd corners in there that I could have wrecked, you know, like those men from Salt Lake were afraid of.

On the morning of the second day, the cornerstone ceremonies were to be held at 10 a.m. and all the people in their white-tops from other towns were there for the conference meeting which was to follow the laying of the cornerstone. And people would come to the blacksmith shop and talk to us and want to know if it was ready and we'd tell them, "Well, no, it isn't ready." But finally we said that yes, it was ready.

Now at five minutes to ten a team of horses was to be provided. We opened the front door and the men had brought a sled and there were enough men that they could lift the stone and carefully put it on the sled. Then, with the team of horses, they dragged the stone over to the corner of the Kanab Stake House to be hoisted by a block and tackle into place and then to be placed with mortar by Apostle Ballard. My brother, Frank, had built and laid in place all the exterior stone and he was present to plumb this cornerstone in the right position as Apostle Ballard made the dedicatory prayer. The sealed metal box was then placed in the center cavity provided for it and the stone was sealed shut with mortar.

President Ballard had just come from Mexico where he'd opened the Mexican Mission and he said that he had seen the engraving of the Aztec artists there and he said, "This man who engraved this stone must have been a descendant of the Aztecs." And there were many cowboys there who had never been to church in their lives. (John Cram had just lost $100 betting that I couldn't engrave that stone; that was the only time he was ever in the chapel.) Anyway, they called me "the Aztec" after that for quite awhile. Gad, I got a kick out of that.

Upon visiting Kanab these memories come back, and upon every occasion I have seen tourists looking at this stone. About four years ago a convert to the Church and his family, wife and four children, had had car trouble and had been towed to the garage near there. They were taking a picture of the stone and I knew they were strangers so I asked if I could be of any assistance and they told me about their car trouble. They wanted me to tell them who the stake president was and where he lived because they needed monetary help before they could proceed on from Seattle to Mesa where they had purchased a home recently. So I took my purse and said, "I'm on my way home from a two-month tour of the East but I have a twenty-dollar bill left, but with my credit card I can get home." And the tourist said, "Who shall I say gave me this money?" I said, "Just say the man who engraved the cornerstone."

Part Six

Spiritual Stories

The Man Who Didn't Die

Now what I wanted to talk to you about was faith because we hear that faith is our religion and on our faith are our testmonies. So I would like to tell you some experiences I have had that are miracles that I've been a part of, or associated with, in one way or another.

Now my faith in the gospel has been built upon first-hand testimonies of associates of the Prophet Joseph. So I have a pretty good foundation in that respect. And I have always had a great deal of faith in the gospel and have exercised a great deal of faith many times which saved my life. We talk about miracles not being performed anymore, but really, I believe that they are, just as much as in the days I'm talking about.

We had one man in Fredonia, Arizona, who had no belief whatever, apparently, didn't belong to any faith, but who was the most prolific profaner that I have ever listened to. Now he would talk with all his sentences mingled with swear words and, of course, that would grate on me because I was taught never to profane. There was only four cars in the country and he had one, and three of us in Kanab had one, and if anything went wrong with any of these four, I had to fuss around with them and put oil in the radiator and see if they'd run.

He came up to Kanab one day in his high-heeled boots, a-walking and a-sweatin' and a-swearing. He came around the corner of the Stockmen's store and we were all sittin' on our heels a-whittlin', which was a common pastime down there, in fact around that post office there was about three inches of shavings. All of them cowboys would do it waiting for the stage to come in and it'd come in; it was a horse-drawn stage. Well, anyway, he came around and we could hear him swearing long before he turned the corner. He came up here about fifty yards and wanted to know where I was and I saw him, I was sitting over there and I said, "What's the matter, Charlie?" His name was Charlie McCornick. I said, "What's the matter, Charlie?" And he took off his hat and wiped the perspiration off and he said–well, I'd tell you what he said but it'd take twenty words, including the swear words–but he said, "I was coming over the Halfway Hill," and of course a lot of swear words, "and this car wouldn't take it in high, so I socked her into intermedium, and the transom fell out." He called the transmission a "transom." And I said, "That's all right, I'll pull it up here and have it fixed for you." But can you imagine, to say those few words, it took him twenty or thirty words with all that profaning.

Well now, we moved out of Kanab in 1928, and in 1930, we went down for a visit to the Grand Canyon and we left there at daylight and thought we'd come through Kanab and say hello to our old family doctor, Doc Norris, and make Richfield that night. It took two days from Salt Lake to Kanab because there was no roads. I was one of the best drivers and I think I was the first driver to drive it in one day, finally. You had to follow around the streams and over the hills down through different canyons as there was no road down there. So, we stopped to see our old family doctor, but he wasn't at home, so I just come off of his porch and said to Romania, "We won't be able to see him. We better go if we're gonna make Richfield tonight." And just as I was stepping into the car, I looked up east from his home and I recognized his car coming around the corner. So I said, "There he is now." We waited for him and he said, boy, he was glad to see us. Asked us how we were and we told him we were in a hurry, that we wanted to go on to Richfield tonight if we could make it. And he said, "Well, I'd like you to do me a favor. Charlie McCornick just died about half an hour ago in Fredonia. Will you take his death certificate to Richfield?" We said, "Sure." He said, "I'll hurry as fast as I can." He went into his office and wrote this death certificate out for Charlie McCornick, put it in an envelope and addressed it to the Bureau of Vital Statistics down in Flagstaff, Arizona, Coconino County. He said he'd appreciate it if we'd mail that because the stage had gone. So we took the letter and, after we got in our hotel, I went out across the street and mailed this death certificate for Charlie McCornick.

Well, there was no communication between us and those people. And two years later when coming out of the Tabernacle in Salt Lake City, after the priesthood meeting at night (and you know how they were jammed in those days; even now you can't get a seat), I was coming out there and someone tapped me on the shoulder and I looked over my shoulder and it was Charlie McCornick. So I knocked these first two men down and pretty near knocked the other three ahead of them down. I knew I carried Charlie's death certificate, and I knew him so well because of the way he talked; well, I knew him better than I know my own brother because of the characteristics of his face and the way he talked and so forth. Well, anyway, when I got stopped by these men in front of me, why I looked over toward Charlie, and the man right by him was holding up his hand and he was Bishop Judd of Kanab and he said, I knew him so well, he said, "It's all right, Rowland, this is Charlie." He says, "It's all right, you can stop now," so I did. But I wouldn't shake hands with Charlie. I was afraid to shake hands with him but I shook hands with Bishop Judd and he says, "It's all right, Charlie's my first counselor." Now imagine, here he was, his first counselor. And Doc Norris in Kanab, the best doctor in the country, had sewed Charlie up and told his wife to take him home, that nothing could be done for him and let him die in peace. And so this was the event when she called Doc Norris down there to witness that Charlie was dead and sign his death certificate.

So last fall, in order to get some books, some information for Deirdre and get pictures to authenticate some of these crazy stories I'm telling you, I got his wife's picture. She's ninety-three, her name's Martinie McCornick and when she saw me, of course she

cried 'cause she knew that I knew this thing had happened. Now I'm talking about miracles, or healings–Martinie McCornick had to go, she couldn't drive the car, no one else there could in that town, so she had to go four city blocks by foot, and they're long, they're all laid out by Brigham Young, four blocks to get Bishop Judd and if she found him right at home or out in the garden I don't know. But anyway, they had to walk back down there four blocks and Bishop Judd laid his hands upon Charlie's head and brought him back to life. And he lived twenty-five years and of course I have his monument now with the date he died, a picture of it, you know. Well that's really a miracle.

Praying for Rain

Now we had drought like we have down there this year, and the cattlemen's and sheepmen's stock were all dying. I have had to shoot, I don't say hundreds, but nearly hundreds of cows because they were down and they couldn't get up and it was just an act of mercy to destroy them by shooting them. And they'd come in from the range and go down into the water hole and tank up with water and then they couldn't get back out, and that was the end of them.

So Kanab's stake president, W. W. Seegmiller, who one time run to be a candidate for governor, called a fast meeting to see if we could do anything about this drought that the cattle and sheep were dying of. The whole economy of that country was cattle and sheep. Oh, they had a few alfalfa fields to feed the horses, but that was all. And so all the Saints (of course there was a lot of people who weren't LDS, quite a lot, oh, not very many, but some), all the Saints called this special fast meeting. And the president of the stake asked Asa Judd, who was the bishop down there, this man I'm telling you about that brought this Charlie McCornick back to life, and he was to be the mouth for the prayer.

And of course the whole hall was filled with people. And some of the unbelievers also was there, and I know that some of them bet gold that it wouldn't do any good to have this fast meeting. They was always betting, one way or the other, and they didn't have any checks so it was always gold. One man especially, I call him High-pockets, he was six foot six, he'd always bet against the Church, but another little fellow called Gid Findlay, he was a short fellow, had the best horses in the country, and he'd always bet with us, he always bet with the Saints. So they'd get a third party to hold the gold, you know. But anyway, some bet that this fast wouldn't do a bit of good, this Highpockets and I don't know how many others, quite a lot of others did too, just for the heck of it.

But, anyway, when Bishop Judd got up there to pray, I think it was one of the most inspiring prayers that I can remember, and I have heard the authorities[50] pray many times, but I have never heard anything like this. Everything physical seemed to disappear. Everything was spiritual. A woman was playing the organ but there was no organ there. She was just settin' there, you know, that's the way it looked. And all those people setting up on the stand, the horse beaters and everyone else (the high councilmen were all horse beaters you know, but they would have them sitting up there on the stand), well there was no chairs.

Well, anyway, the result was that it began to rain. And it didn't only rain, but it snowed, and it didn't only snow and rain, but a terrible windstorm came up, and it plowed snow into windrows for miles, twenty-five or thirty miles beyond the water holes, so that all these starving cattle and sheep could now go out and they could stay there until the fifteenth of May and get plenty of forage. See, they'd cleaned up every bite to eat within the range they could walk before, from the waterholes. But now the Saints had saved all that were still left of the cattle and sheep, so it was a great day of rejoicing.

So that is one of the greatest testimonies that I have, to know that the Lord really answers prayers.

The Gift of Tongues

Now another miracle I'll tell that I've witnessed. My neighbor, who lived catty-cornered across the street from our home, and whose daughter was about the same age as my next youngest sister, who was three years older than I was, was possessed of evil spirits. I had actually seen her perform with an axe and she could drive that axe

[50]General Authorities of the Mormon Church.

into a tree until she couldn't pull it out and neither could her brother. He was older by six or eight years than I was. So the bishop, who was the father of J. Spencer Cornwall, who led the Mormon Choir for so many years, maybe some of you've heard of him, he sent the deacons and ward teachers to every L.D.S. family in that ward to have a fast meeting and a prayer meeting for this poor sister. By the way, she was the sister of his first counselor in the bishopric. So we all met on the special fast day and our church was crowded. I think everyone in the ward was anxious to do what the bishop had advised them to do, to fast and to pray for this Sister Williams.

Now, as soon as the sacrament was passed, the bishop said, "It's time for your testimonies," and naturally he bore his testimony. And then he set down. And my Sunday school teacher, who sat about six or eight seats from me on the same row, got up and she was possessed of, I guess, the Spirit of the Holy Ghost, because she was as white as snow and she talked in tongues, not just a few words but a lot of words, and then sat down. And of course the audience was deathly quiet, you know, and they expected to hear the translation of the tongues and we set there under this tension for maybe two or three minutes and the bishop stood up again and he said, "Does anyone have the interpretation of Sister Lenora Murphy's tongue?" And

no one stood up. So he said, "We will ask the Lord for the interpretation." So he prayed, a simple prayer, and as soon as he sat down, another friend of mine, especially of my mother's, got up and interpreted word for word what Lenora Murphy had said. Now the fact was made known by the interpreter that our prayers had been answered, that Sister Williams was well. As soon as she set down, the bishop dismissed the meeting and talked to his first counselor and the counselor invited the entire ward to come down if they would like to, down to Williams's home. And they had a large home and big trees out in front of it and a big lawn, set back quite a ways from the road.

So the bishop asked Spencer Cornwall, his son, to bring the ward quartet and I was in the ward quartet. So we went down, and by the time we got there, George Williams, the first counselor, had driven ahead and they had brought chairs out and set them on the front porch so they had the whole family out there including this girl, you know, just as well as she ever had been. So we all shook hands with her and then the quartet sang "Master the Tempest is Raging." We did have a pretty good quartet, we sang all over Salt Lake Valley. Then we had someone close the meeting with a thankful prayer for what we'd witnessed, and then Spencer asked the quartet if we would sing "Till We Meet Again." And as we sang that, when we got to the chorus, he motioned to the entire crowd to sing. I think that was the most inspirational prayer I've ever heard, because I believe that a song is a prayer, by really dedicated Saints, when sung with the proper tone and at the proper time. And neighbors for miles around could hear that song in that quiet evening, those people sang with such spirit. And I've never heard anything like it. It always reminded me of the time when Christ was born when the angels sang to the shepherds and the people of Bethlehem.

So that's another testimony to me that the gospel which we're engaged in is true beyond any shadow of a doubt. And I might say, too, I never repeated the words of those tongues, but I remember what my teacher was saying. I couldn't interpret them, but I knew those words, I carried them with me without telling them to anyone all my life. Then I had my testimony strengthened many years later when I heard those same words in our temple. So that's been one of the biggest, greatest, strongest testimonies to me, this gift of tongues which I personally witnessed and which I had a part in, in the singing, when people went to witness themselves that a miracle had been performed. I knew a lot of them already knew it had taken place. I did. I don't think they went for that purpose. I thought they just went down there to show how grateful they were to this family that the Lord had made their daughter well.

The Scotsman Who Couldn't Die

My father was the only one of his family in England that joined the Church. But on my mother's side, there's her father and mother, and her two brothers joined. Her father was a Scotsman and he came to this country and he wouldn't go get his temple work done. He was kinda stubborn; I think those Scots people are. Anyway, we was out right across the road from the Cottonwood Mall there now and I can still see the old rock pillars there where he was killed; he was hauling hay and his team of horses ran away and threw him between the hay rack and one of those pillars and crushed him. I laugh when I think about this because we went up to their home there in Cottonwood on the day of the funeral service. They couldn't keep the bodies very long because they had no morticians in those days, so this was the morning of the third day and Grandpa was prepared for burial. And they were going to take him to the ward chapel, which was two or three blocks from his home, and everyone was sitting around in there. But all of a sudden, Grandpa raised up out of the coffin–and I went out the door and right on through the rail that went around the porch; I took that with me. So a runner was sent to the chapel to tell the people Grandpa was alive again.

And Grandpa said, now I've heard him say this, he said, "Those people–." Let me digress a little bit. Since that time I've thought that going fom Utah to Wyoming, crossing that state line, or going from Utah to Arizona, you know, there's no difference. And there's no difference between mortality and immortality; it's all the same you know. And this is why I'm telling you this–it's just exactly the same. He said, "You know, Rowland," he's a Scotsman and I can't talk like he did, but he said, "I could see all my friends, and I called them by name and they called me by name." But he said, "I talked to my friends and they were too busy to talk to me outside of saying 'hello.' They all had plenty to do." "And anyway," he said, "they told me to come back. I had to come back and do this temple work."

But he wouldn't do it. He was stubborn just like I say, and I guess he wanted to live forever. But one day, we got a telegram down to Kanab, and my mother was to come and go through the Salt Lake Temple with him as soon as she could. So I took her to the railroad in Marysvale, that was 130 miles from Kanab, further than that in those days the way we had to go. But I put her on the train there and she came up here and they went down to the temple. And they did this specific work that he'd been assigned to do, that they sent him back to do from the spirit world, and he did that and he said, "Mary, my work is finished, goodbye." He closed his eyes, and that was it. So that was the end of my grandfather, Dudley McDonald.

And he's the man who established the honeybee farms up in the Cottonwood area in Salt Lake Valley. He was a horticulturist, and a good one because those peach orchards up there, boy, are they full of the choicest fruit of any in the valley and they still are budded from those same McDonald trees that he raised and grafted and grew.

C. V. Anderson

Let me tell you about my friend, C. V. Anderson, who in 1905 or '06 originated the famous mica axle grease which was sold to farmers throughout the intermountain region, to practically every farmer in the entire area, as a lubricant for their machinery. And every wagon owner owned a can of this and had it in his jockey box[51] so he could grease his wagon wheels at night when he was on freighting trips, and so forth. All the farm machinery was also lubricated with this axle grease which later became famous.

Andy Anderson was this man's name. He was a Danish man and he spoke broken. He lived in a little village at the north end of Cache Valley, near the town of Preston, Idaho. This was only a small village and they had a schoolhouse and used the schoolhouse for the

[51]Rider explained that a jockey box was "just above the farmer's foot support that went across in front of the wagon box."

church services. And every year Andy would go into the hills east of Preston and get quaking asp poles to furnish fuel for the wood stove in this schoolhouse so that it would be warm for the church services. And for this service, the bishop of this little ward gave him credit on his tithing receipts. And every time he'd go to church and the bishop would give him this receipt for his labor, he'd put his arms around Andy and say, "Andy, you're a good man." And Andy would smile, he was rather bashful, nod his head, and he thought that was good compensation, to have a good man like the bishop tell him that he was a good man.

So on one of these trips to the canyon to procure this wood, as he drug the poles down the mountainside and went up with his snake horse[52] to drag more poles down, he noticed going up the drag trail that he had uncovered a deposit of some strange material that he wasn't familiar with. So on his trip down, he gathered some of this and put it in his coat and pant's pockets and when he got back to town, he thought someday he would go down to the Agricultural College in Logan and see someone in the geology department about it. And my instructor, William Petersen, was the head of that department and I attended his classes in geology and also took field trips with him. And Andy went to him for an examination of this material that he had found. And Professor Petersen told him it was mica and he said it had excellent lubricating qualities.

So this gave Andy an idea; if he could combine this mica deposit with some kind of conveyor that it would mix with, he would have a good product for lubricating his wagon wheels and his farm machinery. And so he had the inspiration to do this thing and every spare moment of his time when he wasn't out working his farm, after work and at nights, he would build a fire in his little blacksmith shop adjoining his barn and he would try to mix this mica with lard and with suet from the beef that he'd killed and various other fatty substances to keep it together. But he never had any luck. He tried and tried and tried.

So he was to Sacrament meeting on fast day at the little schoolhouse and heard several of the people get up and bear their testimonies to the truthfulness of the gospel. Quite a few of them, sever-

---

[52]A snake horse was "a horse which was hooked to a log chain to 'snake out' [drag along the ground] the dry quaking asp poles."

al of them anyway, said that their prayers were answered. And they believed the Lord did answer their prayers. So Andy's wife that night said, "Andy, why don't you pray about this matter you've been working on so many months, and maybe the Lord will answer your prayer. I'm sure he will," she said, "if you're sincere about it."

So they decided to pray about it and they did and the next evening after work, after he came in from the field work, he built his fire in the forge in his blacksmith shop and he put on some pig fat and rendered it out, then went and got several handfuls of this mica. He had collected a big lot of it; went up with a wagon and got a lot of it and brought it down, you know, several bushels of it, several burlap bags of it. So he took a couple of handfuls and put it in this hot fat and he stirred it in and stirred it in, and he'd done this same thing for a long while, several months. And every time he'd thought it was right, he'd take it off the fire and let it cool, and when it cooled it separated. It wouldn't coagulate with the fat, see. And it would be no good, of course, as something to sell to the farmers for a lubricant.

This night, though, when he went through all this process again, probably for the 500th time, he thought, "Oh, boy, now my prayers will be answered." And he had the mica and the hot fat all mixed thoroughly and it looked grand just like it always had done. And he set it over in the window to cool, and he kept watching it and as it got cool, why it did just like all the other experiments he had made. It separated and, of course, was a failure. So, he was so mad at thinking he had asked the Lord to help him solve this that he took the whole pail and he threw it down on the shop floor with all his might, and it scattered all over the floor. And he looked at it and he saw in great big, foot-high letters, "C.V." And he said, "For heaven's sake. That must be the answer to my prayers." In his broken Danish he thought "C" was for "K," "keep"; and "V" was for "W," "wigglin'." So "C.V." stood for "Keep Wiggling," or "Keep Vigglin'." And he gathered the mica and fat all up and he put it in the pot and put it on the fire again. He kept stirring it and, as it cooled, he kept wiggling the pot. And sure enough, it coagulated. And that's the origination of mica axle grease. And they called him "C.V. Anderson" forever, all over this country, after that.

But now then he sold the grease to the farmers; all his neighbors come to get it. And it was a great lubricant. Oh, they never had any more squeaks in their axles, in all the farm machinery or in their wagons. And due to mouth to mouth advertising, from one farmer to another, word got scattered all over the valley about it. So people would come in in their white-tops to get a supply of it, in buckets, in large buckets, in any kind of a convenience to carry it in. Anderson couldn't make it fast enough, so he put a little shed on the side of the blacksmith shop to make this. And then, of course, he'd go up in the mountains to get a supply of the mica but no one knew where he got it. And then he got a can company somewhere in Missouri to make a certain can with a lid on it. And it held a pound of this mica axle grease. And every farmer in the whole country here's familiar with these cans because they had "Mica Axle Grease" written around on these white cans and they only held a pound and they were convenient for the farmers to carry in their jockey boxes.

Well, then Andy went to church and he paid his tithing, not with labor, but with cash now. He was getting lots of money now. See, at the stake conference down at Logan, the farmers all told each other about this mica axle grease and many salesmen came to get the opportunity and the privilege to distribute it all over their territories, wherever they'd travel, you know, to all the mercantile stores all over the farming area. And so Andy Anderson built up a tremendous business and, of course, he paid a big tithing check and then the bishop would put his arm around him and say, "C. V., you're a good, *good* man."